THOSE THREE WORDS

THOSE THREE WORDS

A birth mother's story of choice, chance, & motherhood

CHRISTINE BAUER

Those Three Words © copyright 2018 by Christine Bauer. All rights reserved. No part of this book may be reproduced in any form whatsoever, by photography or xerography or by any other means, by broadcast or transmission, by translation into any kind of language, nor by recording electronically or otherwise, without permission in writing from the author, except by a reviewer, who may quote brief passages in critical articles or reviews.

ISBN 13: 978-1-63489-230-8
Library of Congress Catalog Number: 2018935096
Printed in the United States of America
First Printing: 2018
23 22 21 20 19   6 5 4 3 2

Page design by Mayfly Design and typeset in the Whitman and Filosofia typefaces

Minneapolis, MN
www.wiseink.com

DEDICATION

To my mother, whose kindness, compassion, and love taught me everything I needed to know to be a good mom and good human being. I miss you and wish that you could be here to hold this book in your hands; I know you're watching from above.

To Becky, my sister, best friend, and lifelong seatmate on this rollercoaster of life. Thank you for helping me bring Katie into this world and for connecting the dots to make it all come together.

To Katie, my beautiful daughter, you are my sunshine and the reason for all of this. You make my life complete, and the world is a better place because you are in it. It was all meant to be.

To Remy Mae, my granddaughter, you are a blessing and you completed the circle of life for me. I hope you never lose your curiosity, confidence, and candor, and that you always have the right to choose. Live fearlessly, my love.

To Cindy, the best "other mother" out there, and Dennis, the super-duper dad. Thank you for being such wonderful parents and for letting Katie know all along that she had two mamas.

To my son Dylan, for your fun spirit and your love, and for providing me with enough parenting adventures and stories to fill another book. As they say: everything is copy.

To my son Jared, thanks for being such a wonderful, easy kid and my biggest cheerleader, for always asking how the writing was going and telling me: "You can do it, Mom."

To birth mothers everywhere, for your strength, courage, and bravery.

THOSE THREE WORDS

CHAPTER 1

Late September 1984

Overdose Warning. My index finger landed on these two words. I tilted the box to reduce the fluorescent lights' glare as it flickered across the small typeface.

Once the words came into focus, I scanned them quickly:

TYLENOL® PM relieves your pain fast so you can sleep and feel refreshed after a good night's rest.

I didn't want an overdose warning; I wanted overdose advice. I wanted to know what to take so I would sleep for an eternity.

I would need to take more than just the Tylenol to be sure it worked, so I decided I should combine the pills with Nyquil. Yes, together, these would create my own little annihilation cocktail.

But would buying these two products together look suspect at the checkout counter? The cashier could ask, "*Hey, girl, are you planning to kill yourself?*"

And then I could say: "*Yes, you asshole, I am. I'm pregnant and I'm desperate and this is the solution that causes the least pain for everyone in the long run.*"

"*And it's none of your fucking business,*" I'd add.

One by one, I took the packages off the shelf—two of each—and placed them gently in the red plastic shopping basket draped across my left arm.

"Excuse me," a middle-aged lady said suddenly, startling me. She smiled and nodded at me. I stepped aside so she could reach out and take her own box of sleep aids from the shelf. I was sure she was really going to use hers to sleep and not to kill herself, but I guess you never know.

As I moved over for her, I reached deep down inside my soul and pulled out a smile in return. I hadn't smiled for days, but this woman made me think of my mom, whose gentle face entered my mind like an uninvited but welcome guest.

I meandered through the drugstore aisles. Before now I'd never thought much about the number of products that were available to solve your problems. There were products to take away body odor, products to make your skin soft, products to get rid of zits and stop bleeding. There were tablets to freshen your breath and capsules to make your headache go away. There were pills to make you sleep, and even to kill yourself if you wanted.

But there was nothing to make a pregnancy disappear.

As I passed the plethora of feminine hygiene supplies, I thought of the pretty pink box of Playtex tampons that sat unopened in my dorm-room closet. It had taunted me over the past few weeks, especially this morning. I'd thought of the many times over the years that I'd hated having to open those boxes, having to deal with the inconvenience and hassle of a period. Now opening that box would seem like opening a very special gift.

I moved on from tampons to chips. I stood in a daze in front of the Doritos, Fritos, Old Dutch potato chips, and other unhealthy snacks. The bags lounged in their steel racks, just waiting to be picked up. The Fritos looked good—they always looked good—so I grabbed a bag, placing it strategically into my basket to cover the boxes of Tylenol and Nyquil. I also grabbed some Doritos. *What the hell? I may as well eat all I want.* I'd been dieting for years—most of my life, really. Another curse of being a girl, and a childhood gymnast at that.

As I approached the checkout counter, the collage of women's magazines reinforced the ideal body image that had bombarded me most of my life. Headlines blared: "Lose 10 pounds in 2 weeks!" "Get a flat tummy fast!" "Thinner thighs in 30 days!" None of that mattered anymore.

The guy at the counter was about my age, and I was relieved that he didn't seem fazed by my strange combination of items—I threw in a Toblerone chocolate bar at the last minute to add to the mix as he rang up the sale.

"Thanks," I said, avoiding his eyes. I didn't want this guy to feel bad later on when the authorities figured out he was the one who sold me the ingredients for my permanent nightcap.

Plastic bag clutched tightly in my hand, I headed back out to the outdoor mall area of downtown Mankato, Minnesota. I took a seat on one of the wooden benches that dotted the sidewalk and dug my Marlboro Lights out of my backpack. It was about my tenth cigarette for the day, and it wasn't even noon. I lit up and took a deep, long drag.

God, I hoped this was the right way to do this. *This is not something I can screw up; I don't want to screw up again.* But I was damned either way. "Thou shalt not kill," the commandment said. Nowhere did it specify, "Thou shalt not kill yourself," but the nuns had made it clear: you do that and you'll burn in hell. But what made them know everything? Hell, the church didn't even respect them, so why should I?

Maybe a gun would be a better choice than pills. There were plenty at home, as I came from a family of hunters. I pictured myself back at home, unlocking the gun cabinet and taking a shotgun from the rack. I'd sneak back to my bedroom, position myself on the bed with the yellow-and-green daisy-print bedspread. Then I'd pull the trigger. It would be fast. And it was more of a sure thing.

But it would be so awful for whoever would find me—and unfortunately, that person would most likely be my mom. She was always home. *Always there for us.*

I put my head in my hands and rubbed my temples, careful not to burn my hair with my cigarette. No, I couldn't do that. My mom was just too nice and too sweet for me to do that to her. To find her baby like that would be awful—red blood and grey matter with bits of blonde hair splattered against the beautiful daisy bedspread.

I took another deep drag and looked up. The sign "Someplace Else" hung there, laughing at me.

Just last week, my new friends and I had been in Someplace

Else, one of the more happening bars downtown. Laughing, dancing, talking, flirting—we'd been on top of the world that night, the same as every night since school had begun. It was a dream come true, being at college and on my own.

Now here I was at the same spot, this time at bottom. In just a few weeks I had tumbled from standing on the high board of life to lying at the bottom of the pool. Just last week I was a freshman in love with my friends and my new life. Now, I sat here wondering how many sleeping pills I should take to end my life.

I'd already sorted through my options.

Option 1: Give up college. Get married. Live in Mitchell. Be a mom.

Option 2: Have the baby. Be a single parent. Live with my parents in the town I had so desperately wanted to leave.

Option 3: Have an abortion. Don't tell anyone. Ever. Go on with life.

Option 4: Grow the baby. Have the baby. Give it to some strangers to raise.

But none of these seemed right. It also didn't even seem right that I was having to make this decision at all. I had used birth control. I had only slept with Jim, my boyfriend from back home, about five times—that wasn't much! Especially not compared to all my friends. But here I was. Which is how I ended up at Option 5.

CHAPTER 2

It all began with a phone call.

"How long does it take to get a pregnancy test?" I said softly into the phone, my heart pounding so hard I could feel it on my skin. My stomach churned rapidly, and I had to suppress the vomit that kept creeping up my throat, threatening to erupt.

"It will take about an hour," the woman replied coolly. "We just need a urine sample."

"Can I come in today? Now?" I asked, struggling to hold the receiver with my sweaty, shaking hands.

"Yes," she said flatly, like she got these calls from scared college students every day.

Student Health Services was in the building next to mine, conveniently connected by a hallway on the way to my first class. "Okay, I'll be there soon," I said, and managed to get the phone back in its cradle.

I quickly finished getting ready and then took the time for a cigarette. I cranked my window out as far as it would go and hopped up on the counter that wrapped around the front of our fourteen-square-foot dorm room. I curled my legs up to my chest and hugged them, savoring each deep drag, carefully blowing smoke out the window as I watched students walking to class on this crisp September morning.

Some students were scurrying alone, hurrying to their classes. Others walked slowly, chatting with friends. But they all looked like they hadn't a care in the world; they were just enjoying their life on campus. That had been me the first two weeks of school. I loved college—everything about it. I loved the freedom and independence of being away from home. I loved my classes. I loved learning. I loved being known for just being *me*—not someone's little sister or daughter, not someone who belonged to this group or that. I was free to be me.

I wiped away the tear that was slowly meandering down my cheek and took one last long drag on my Marlboro Light. *Time to go.*

With my head bowed low, I walked quickly down the hallway. I'd hoped to avoid contact, but I couldn't. There were too many people around.

"Hey, how ya doin'?" asked Cathy, my across-the-hall neighbor, as I sped toward the exit.

"Great," I replied. "Just on my way to grab something to eat before class." What I really wanted to do was scream and cry and yell at her: "I'm on my way to Health Services for a fucking pregnancy test."

Only a few people sat in the waiting room. It was filled with cheaply upholstered chairs and littered with health information brochures: "What You Need to Know About STDs." "Recognizing Depression."

Sheepishly, I walked up to the receptionist and stood before her.

"Yes?" she asked.

I suspended myself on tiptoes, leaning over the counter. "Ahhh, I'm here for a pregnancy test," I whispered.

"What's that?" she asked.

My eyes darted to the other people in the room. I leaned in again and said, just a bit louder, "I'm here for the pregnancy test. I called a little bit ago?"

"Oh," she said curtly, grabbing a pen and clipboard and pushing them toward me with an uncaring gaze. "Okay, you need to fill this out."

I took the seat farthest from any of the other attendees and began filling in the information: name, address, birthdate. In just a few weeks I would turn nineteen.

When I'd completed the form, I got up and handed it back to the receptionist, who I now realized not only acted but *looked* a bulldog with her square jaw and protruding lower lip. I sat back down.

Even though I was waiting to be called, I jumped when I heard my name. I got up and walked quickly to meet the nurse, who at least smiled when she greeted me. I followed her back to the exam area; she got my height and weight and then asked me for a urine sample.

As I closed the bathroom door, nausea swept over me again. I sat on the cold, hard toilet seat and dutifully peed into the plastic cup. This alone felt violating, so seeing the stirrups on the exam table in the next room made me shiver.

The nurse smiled again. "So you believe you're pregnant. How late is your period?" Her voice was calm.

"Well, I was supposed to get it on September 7, the day school started," I explained.

"Were you using birth control?"

"Yes, I was. The Today Sponge. Every time." I repeated, "Every time," as if it would somehow help.

"So you are about two weeks late. Any tenderness in your breasts?" she asked.

I hesitated. "No, not really," tumbled out of my mouth, even though my boobs had been tender, tingly, hurting.

"Well, it could very well be nervousness from starting school and moving away from home. That's all pretty big and stressful stuff, and our bodies react to that stress. We'll run this test and then have it back in an hour."

"Sure. Thanks," I mumbled as I grabbed my backpack and headed out the door.

I had time for a cigarette before class, which happened to be in the basement of the same building. I stepped out the back door, lit a cigarette, and began to pray:

"Dear God, don't let me be pregnant. Please, *please* don't let this happen to me. I want to finish school. I want to get a good job and to explore the world. I want to make new friends. Please, God, I don't want to be a mom right now. I can't be a mom right now. And I don't want to disappoint my parents. I've already disappointed them enough. Please, God, I won't ask for anything ever again. I know I've said that before, but this is really the last time I ask for anything. Really. Please, God."

I flicked my cigarette down and ground it out beneath my foot.

I ran my fingers through my hair and popped a piece of gum in my mouth. *Pull it together,* I told myself as I headed to class.

I strode into Women's Studies 101 and slipped into a chair, glad that today they were arranged in straight rows rather than the usual circle. This was my favorite class, even though before coming to MSU I had never even heard of "Women's Studies." From the very first day, I loved it. I loved learning about women's history, how we had overcome—or were overcoming—oppression. How we had earned our rights to vote, to work, to make our voices heard, to have control over our bodies.

Every day I sat in this class, I wondered why all this important information hadn't been taught in high school. We all could have benefited from this. Why didn't I realize the ads I'd grown up seeing were so sexist, so degrading? I knew they made me uncomfortable, but I could never pinpoint why. I had taken for granted so much about how far women had come, and I hadn't understood how far we had yet to go.

Jesus, maybe I wouldn't be sitting here waiting for the results of a pregnancy test if I'd had more women's studies as a teenager. Maybe I would have been more focused on myself and my dreams than whether I had a boyfriend, or looked good, or was skinny enough.

Hearing the word "orgasm" brought me back from my own thoughts to the Crawford Hall Green Room.

"The majority of men have an orgasm every time they have sex," Patty, our professor, said. "Yet some women go through their whole lives—including pregnancy and childbirth—without having even one. How sad is that, huh?"

What she said next was even worse. "I know of women who have had ten, twelve children and lived into their eighties and never had an orgasm, which I think is more common than we know."

Mary, the smart-looking brunette with neat, cropped hair who sat just a few feet away from me, didn't hesitate to express her frustration. "Well, how do you know if you have or haven't? I think I may have, but I'm not sure."

"Oh, you'll know," said Ann, the middle-aged, self-described "ex-housewife."

Nervous laughter erupted from around the room. Mary was not alone.

"I can't help but feel really angry," Mary sputtered in return. "Here I have a child and I've never had an orgasm. I had to go through pregnancy and childbirth, and now I'm a single mom bearing the child-rearing responsibilities, and I've never gotten the full benefits of sex. It sucks, especially knowing my ex has had tons of them. It really sucks. It's not fair."

Silence blanketed the classroom for what felt like minutes.

God, that could be me, I thought. *Pregnant and not even having had the big O.* And, oh, the irony of it all—that we should be having this discussion on this day, as I waited to learn my fate.

Class went too slow and too fast at the same time. Before I knew it, I was back at Health Services to learn my destiny. The same nurse greeted me back, but this time her smile seemed different. Or maybe I was just paranoid. I followed her down the short hallway and took a seat in the hard, plastic chair next to the plain, steel desk. It was all so sterile, cold, uncaring.

She took a seat at the desk, flipped open my chart, and paused for a second. Then her eyes moved slowly from the paper to meet mine.

"Well, Christine, your test is positive."

My mind raced. *What does she mean, "positive?" Positive, I'm pregnant? Positive, I'm not? What is she saying? God, help me. Oh my God. Oh shit. I know what she's saying.*

My face became red hot; I could feel the color burning its way up my pale cheeks. Soon it felt like they were on fire. My head pounded. I felt dizzy.

Then she said those three words: "You are pregnant."

The words hit me with the force of a rear-end collision. I had seen it coming toward me in the rearview mirror, but there was no time to prepare, no way to brace for the impact.

My body thrust forward as I put my head in my hands and folded my head and chest into my lap. "Oh, God," I cried out. And then the tears came; they came from deep within me, from my womb, my gut, my chest. Tears were streaming down my burning face as I struggled to let the shock of it all sink in.

The nurse gently put her hand on my back as I cradled myself in my own lap. "I know it's a shock, Christine, and not the news you were hoping for."

I stayed in that semi-fetal position for a few minutes and then slowly rose up to face the nurse, looking at her with blurred vision and clouded mind.

"According to information you gave us about your last period, you're around six weeks pregnant."

I starred at her as my mind raced. I struggled to find words—but none were right. No words came out. Just tears.

"We have a very good counseling service right across the hall, and I've already asked one of the counselors to speak with you, okay?"

The room was still and sterile except for the sound of crying.

"It's going to be okay," she said after a few minutes. "It might not seem like it now, but it will be okay."

She let me sit a bit longer, letting the news penetrate and sink in. Then she gently reached down and laid her hand on mine, prompting me to stand up.

Like a wounded puppy, I followed her to a small, cramped office where a young woman waited for us. She attempted to shake my hand, but I stood still, hands at my sides, stiff and unmoving. The counselor handed me a Kleenex and began laying out my options.

It was over. I sat in silence for a few more minutes in her office, taking advantage of her Kleenex and catching my breath. And when I finally felt that I could breathe, really breathe, I grabbed my backpack and stood up.

"I have to go. I have to get out of here."

CHAPTER 3

I lay on the lofted twin bed in my dorm room, clutching the goods from the drugstore. Thank God my roommate Judi hadn't been there when I'd returned. I was a mess—exhausted from crying, exhausted from walking down and back up the long hill, and most of all exhausted from the weight of the heavy truth that I was now carrying.

The truth was that I had screwed up again. I couldn't stand the thought of disappointing my parents—and disappointing myself. I'd finally gotten my shit together, and they'd been so happy to see me off to college—*I* had been so happy. How could I do this to them, to me?

As I thought of my mom and dad, my mind turned to my home. Even though I'd been so excited to move out, I loved our home. I pictured the daisy-print bedspread from when I was little. It matched the material on the canopy top of my twin bed. It was such a lovely little girl's bedroom, with its green shag carpet, warm yellow paint, and floor-to-ceiling windows along one wall.

1007 Mitchell Boulevard was a wonderful place to grow up. Our ranch-style home sat on a wide, quiet street in the small town of Mitchell, South Dakota, population 11,000. My hometown's claim to fame: Home of the World's Only Corn Palace. I was Bauer kid number four—the baby of the family—and shared my bedroom with my sister Becky, six years my senior.

Our nightly ritual on Mitchell Boulevard began with reading time, when all four of us kids would crowd into one of the beds to listen to my mom read to us. In her soft and steady voice, she would bring to life the words from books like *Mary Poppins* and *Winnie-the-Pooh*. We would snuggle next to her, draping our small, agile limbs over hers and listening intently as she transported us to the Hundred Acre Wood through her flowing words. We hung on to each word as tightly as we hung on to her, loving what they did for us—loving what *she* did for us.

After half an hour or so of the calm hum of her voice, we'd reluctantly scatter to our beds and wait for our turn at nightly backrubs. We'd drift off to sleep with our minds and bodies full of love.

My mom was the best mom ever.

And at that instant, thinking of her, I knew I couldn't kill myself. I loved her too much. I loved my dad too much. I loved my siblings, my friends, my dogs too much. I loved them all too much to hurt them this way.

These were the same thoughts and feelings that had stopped me the first time too; back in junior high I had also considered taking my life. It was during the time when I careened from a happy-go-lucky, confident, high-achieving girl to a depressed, confused, anxious teen. I hated myself. I hated life. But I loved my family and friends.

They saved me then and now, and they didn't even know it.

CHAPTER 4

The Tylenol PM and Nyquil went untouched, but the Doritos and Fritos were polished off a few days after I bought them by me and my friends—friends who didn't have a clue that anything was wrong, even though I was tormented on the inside. I told no one at school that I was pregnant. I vowed to put on a big act each day until it was over.

And it would be over soon. Jim and I had talked about what to do in numerous phone conversations, but he left the final decision up to me.

"I decided I'm going to have an abortion," I said matter-of-factly. "And you don't even need to go along or worry about it or anything. It'll all be fine."

"Are you sure you don't want to keep the baby?" he asked, quiet desperation in his voice. "I can help you with that too, you know."

"I know, I know. And I appreciate that," I said, twisting the phone cord in my hand. "But I just don't think we're cut out to be parents right now. Do you?"

He paused. "Well, no, not really. But maybe we could make it work."

I turned to make sure Judi wasn't opening the door to come in. "Just 'making it work' isn't good enough for me. I only want to be a parent if I can be the absolute best, and I just don't think I'm up to that right now."

"Well, I have a good job, a stable income. It would be okay."

I had pictured this before, over and over. It had played in my head like a melodramatic movie: Me at home with a baby I had no clue how to care for; Jim going off to his job each day at the local meat-packing plant. Me feeling like a caged animal; he struggling each day with the stress of providing for his family and staying sober.

He had been dry the entire time I'd known him, which by now was about six months. In his drinking days, he'd gotten in many fights, crashed his car, and wrecked some relationships, but I didn't know that side of him. I'd only heard about it. When I met Jim, playing pool at the Corner Pocket Bar, he was only a few months out of rehab. He was shy, polite, and sensitive, a nice guy. He acknowledged his twelve steps many times and was always working to improve himself.

Jim was sweet, and we enjoyed each other's company. But he was not someone I wanted to marry or raise a child with. I'd only wanted to date him for the summer. I'd wanted a boyfriend because all my friends had one.

"Hey, your birthday's next week, isn't it?" he said.

"Yeah, it is. And it's going be terrible." I paused. "That's the day I'm going to do it. That's the day that works for me to go to Sioux Falls." He knew what I meant. That's where I would go to have an abortion. It was one of only two places in South Dakota where you could do that.

"I just want to carry on with my life and my dreams, and this is the best way. I don't think I'd be a great parent right now. Hell, I don't even like babysitting. I've been waiting a long time to get out on my own. I love school, and I want to get a degree and have a career." I was silent for a moment. "I don't want to come back, Jim."

It was quiet again, the pause making its way slowly through the hundreds of miles of phone lines that separated us.

"I understand," he finally said. "And I'll support you however I can."

So it was decided and planned. I would have an abortion in a week. I just had to make it another seven days and pretend nothing was wrong.

CHAPTER 5

October 10, 1984
Pretending was hard. I was not a good actress or a good liar, but tonight, I'd have to put on a very good performance.

Standing at the small sink in our dorm room, I methodically put on my makeup. First, I dabbed on the concealer. I needed lots of it under my eyes; they were dark and puffy from lack of sleep and too many tears. Next, I put on foundation. As I rubbed it into my pale cheeks and forehead, I tried to determine if I looked any different. I turned my head to the right and the left.

Do I look like a pregnant person? Does that glow thing they talk about start right away? Or is that only if you're happy about it? There was certainly no glow. I looked pale, like I'd maybe lost a few pounds. I hadn't felt much like eating.

A little blush and mascara created the finishing touches. I took a few steps over to the radio and turned up the volume to hear Tina Turner: *What's love got to do with it, got to do with it? What's love but a second-hand emotion?* I sang along and grooved a little bit to the music, hoping it would lighten my mood as I dressed for the big event. I had borrowed clothes from my neighbor Robin because I had nothing that would fit this dress code; I put on the lavender skirt and button-down shirt and coordinating multicolor vest, then turned to look in the mirror.

What I saw was an imposter. This preppy look was just not me. The outfit was right for where I was going, though, for pretending everything was okay. No one would ever have to know anything. And it would be over very soon.

As I stood looking in the mirror, I noticed that my boobs already looked bigger. They had been so sore, and already they were growing.

I wore a 32C, so coupled with my five-foot-two frame, they'd already been a good size. But now I was starting to spill out of my bra. I hated it. I hated my body. I hated what was happening. Things were changing too fast. All I wanted to do was climb into my bed, pull the covers over my head, and hide. Instead, I jumped at the knock on my door.

I inhaled deeply and opened the door. There was Jane—also dressed in a preppy skirt and vest, but the look fit her. "Let's go, Chrisy! Time to party, girlfriend."

The wine-and-cheese party was being held at the unofficial house of the fraternity Phi Kappa Psi. It was pledge week, and the sororities and fraternities had been invited to "meet and mingle." I was pledging Alpha Chi Omega. Molly, my childhood friend from home, and a few new friends had essentially talked me into it. I really wasn't the sorority type—I hated cliques—but I was grasping for something, some kind of escape from my reality.

"You will love it," Molly assured me. "The parties are the best, the guys in the frats are the cutest on campus. It's a ton of fun. You totally have to do it."

Molly had been right about so many other things about MSU—she had to be right about this. So there I was, doing it. Because I wanted to be a normal college student. I wanted there to be nothing wrong with me, so I was acting like it. My mom had been so impressed when I told her I was going. "Oh Chrisy, that's wonderful. I'm so happy that everything is going so great!"

I glanced around the room as we walked in. The house, likely built in the early 1900s, had dark hardwood floors and paneling. The sofas and chairs, all pushed to the side, were a bit worn, but the overall effect was impressive, especially compared to some of the other houses I'd been to in Mankato. The house had the smell that old homes do, masked in part by the overabundance of Polo cologne that drifted through the room, wafting off the bodies of the boys dressed in their preppy best. I'd never seen so many Izod, Guess, and Ralph Lauren logos in one room, slithering, hopping, and galloping across vests and shirts.

After quickly sizing up the crowd, I spotted the wine and cheese on the long, narrow table and headed straight for it. "Red or white?" asked the nerdy-looking guy behind the table. I laughed to myself. I'd been asked *Miller or Bud, regular or light,* and *joint or bong* at parties, but never *red or white.*

I grabbed a piece of cheese and a cracker. "I'll take white, please." I thanked him as I took the clear plastic cup from his hand and turned again to survey the room.

The boys were spiffed up in their Sunday best and the girls were looking lovely as well. There was a lot of big and heavily sprayed hair, mine included. Smiles spread easily across the faces in the room. Chatter and laughter brought the decibel level up minute by minute. I raised my hand periodically to wave to familiar faces.

I spotted Tracy and Jeff. They smiled and waved, and I smiled and waved back. Tracy and Jeff were both very cute and nice. Jeff was in my literature class. He was watching me from the corner of his eye and I was doing the same. I think he liked me—and I liked him too, even though I knew that it was wrong. I couldn't help myself. He was tall, about six-foot-two, with blonde hair, blue eyes, and an athletic build. *I bet he played basketball or tennis in high school,* I thought. He looked especially nice tonight in his brown pants, pink dress shirt, and brown sport coat. Perhaps what attracted me to him most was that he exuded such confidence, but not in a cocky way. I couldn't deny it. I had a crush on him.

We'd been talking a lot since we met. We sat by each other in class; he'd lean over and chat with me about an assignment or make comments about the professor. We talked about pledging and the party. He made me feel so normal and so good. I was amazed that a boy that cute and that together might like me.

God, I really liked him, but I knew it was terribly wrong right now. He glanced at me again and made his way over. I felt my face grow hot, a smile forming.

"Hey, Chrisy," he said, with a smile that brought out his dimples and showed his perfectly straight, white teeth. "You sure look nice tonight."

"Why, thank you, Jeff. You look pretty nice yourself." I gave a shy, flirty smile, even though my insides were churning.

We talked for a while, and for just a few minutes I forgot that I was pregnant. I forgot that anything was wrong. I felt happy and normal. I was loving my life again, and it felt so good.

"Hey, everyone," called out our pledge director. "Can I have your attention, please?" People were slow to quiet down, so she whistled. "We're going to play a get-to-know-you game," she shouted. "You have to get to know whomever you're standing next to right now, and then you'll be asked to introduce him or her to the group. So get going."

Jeff and I turned to each other. "I want to get to know you," he said with a boyish grin.

My few minutes of normal and happy were done. I felt embarrassed and self-conscious when he asked me about myself.

I gave him my line about being from the "Home of the World's Only Corn Palace," which made him laugh. I told him that my dad owned and operated Bauer Dental Studio, the largest dental laboratory in South Dakota, while my mother stayed at home. "I'm the youngest of four. My interests in high school were gymnastics and writing and partying."

But of course I didn't tell him, "Oh, yeah, I'm knocked up." I felt like a liar, an imposter.

He told me he was from Minnetonka, a wealthy suburb of Minneapolis. Like mine, his dad owned a business and his mom stayed home. He was the oldest of three and had played on high school football, basketball, and golf teams. He'd had a hard time deciding where to go to school, but ended up at Mankato because it was a party school.

Jeff got me another glass of wine between telling me tidbits about his life. Although I'd never drunk much wine before, it went down easily, too easily. I tried not to feel guilty about drinking it.

I also tried not to feel guilty for liking him. At the end of the party, after many of the guests had dispersed, he led me by my hand up the narrow wooden staircase near the kitchen. I started trembling inside because I liked him so much, but I knew this was wrong.

We stopped outside his bedroom and kissed. It was a tender, slow kiss, but it didn't last long.

"I just can't do this. I have a boyfriend back home that I'm kind of broken up with, but I need to *officially* break up with him." *And I need to officially become un-pregnant*, I thought to myself.

"Well, he'd never know," he whispered, gently touching my face.

"But I would," I said as I turned away to leave. I was not a good liar; I'd have felt terrible if I did something like that.

CHAPTER 6

I was, and still am, a terrible liar. I'm also habitually plagued with guilt, even for the most innocent things. I blame it on being raised Catholic. It must have started around the time of my first confession, for having to confess when I didn't feel I had done anything wrong. What can you do that's so bad by second grade anyway?

We all sat quietly in the row of pews in the small, dimly lit chapel at Holy Spirit Catholic School, lined up alphabetically. Sister Armella and Sister Daniels had put the second-grade class in alphabetical order because no one would volunteer to go first.

"Forgive me, Father, for I have sinned. This is my first confession." We had rehearsed the opening line over and over again. And we knew what we would say for subsequent confessions: "Forgive me, Father, for I have sinned. My last confession was one week ago."

It was supposed to be a good thing, this confession business, but there didn't seem to be anything good about it for me that first time, or any of the times afterward. It was just plain scary. But we didn't have a choice. It was part of being a Catholic and a prerequisite to First Communion. We were all excited about that—everyone was looking forward to finally tasting the wafer after all these years of watching parents and siblings go to communion.

"Christine, keep your feet still," Sister Armella ordered, bringing me back to the moment. I stopped my feet in midswing and brought myself back to the task at hand. Since my feet didn't touch the ground yet or even come close, it was so easy to swing them. And it seemed to calm me down a bit, since I was so nervous.

Gosh, I hope I don't forget my lines when I get in there! And let's see, what was I going to confess again? I was trying to remember my sins when I heard the footsteps.

Click, click, click, click. Father Joyce's footsteps rhythmically pounded the concrete floor of the little chapel. He marched into the room with determination. And although I couldn't see him, I could picture him and his angular features—square jaw, grey flattop, pursed lips. He was on a mission to save our little souls.

I heard a door creak open and shut as he slipped into the confessional in the back of the room. When I heard the door creak open again, I knew it was my turn. As I stood up, my eyes met Sister Armella's and she nodded. It was my signal to proceed. I passed Eve, who had gone before me, as she traveled back to the pew, looking at her long and hard to see if she looked any different now that she was free from sin (at least for a while). She looked exactly the same—big, brown, beautiful eyes; matted, dirty hair; a stained dress that was two sizes too big. *Too bad,* I thought, *all that work for nothing.*

I slowly slipped in and gently closed the door behind me. I knelt down on the cushioned kneeler and tried to ignore the dank, musty smell. My hand shook as I reached up to pull back the little wooden curtain.

I opened it slowly and could make out Father Joyce's profile on the other side of the screen. His head was bowed, leaning into his hand. He looked creepy over there.

I stared at him and began to wonder why I was even in here. Why did Father Joyce have a direct line to God when I didn't? How did sitting on that side of the confessional, wearing a robe, and having people call him "Father" give him a special connection to tell God my sins and ask his forgiveness? I already had my connection to God, and I liked it. I talked to him all the time, especially when I was scared or sad. Why did Father Joyce think he could butt in between me and God?

He cleared his throat. "You may begin."

"Oh, okay," I stammered. "Forgive me, Father, for I have sinned. This is my first confession. Let's see. I have taken the Lord's name in vain. And I have been disrespectful to my mother and father. Or, wait a minute, I have not honored my mother and father. For these and all the sins of my past life I am sorry."

Father didn't say anything right away, and the seconds seemed like minutes. The pause was too long. *Maybe I haven't sinned enough?*

"Oh, I almost forgot. I beared false witness against my neighbor." There, I had one more.

I couldn't really remember doing this. But I thought maybe the more sins the better, especially your first time—like racking up a lot of points in a basketball game.

"Are you sorry for all these sins?" Father asked.

"Yes, I am, Father."

"For your penance, please say three Our Fathers, three Hail Marys, and one Act of Contrition. Now go, in the name of the Father, Son, and Holy Spirit."

"Amen," I said with a sigh of relief. I made the sign of the cross and went back to my pew to say my prayers as instructed. Then I sat back and waited. And waited.

But there was nothing. No great relief. No happy feelings. Nothing. I didn't feel any better or different. Maybe I hadn't said the prayers well enough. I said a few more Hail Marys for good measure.

Once I'd checked off all my prayers, I peeked behind me to see who was going next or returning to their seat. David, in his neatly pressed white shirt and pleated, navy-blue pants, made his way back with a pleasant, satisfied look on his face. Envy washed over me as I gazed at his expression. Clearly, this confession thing had worked on him. He was visibly happy, and I was a little jealous about that.

Even though I didn't get much out of that first confession or subsequent confessions, I was forced to go throughout grade school and into my junior high years. The older I got, the less frequently I went, and eventually I just quit going. I preferred my direct conversations with God and always knew the difference between right and wrong, good and evil.

My strong moral compass was what guided me. Instilled, strengthened, and nurtured by my parents, it never let me veer too far off course. Even though I'd done a lot of stupid things in my life, my internal compass always directed me to my true north.

CHAPTER 7

October 1984
Who the fuck are these people? And why aren't they minding their own business?

I was sitting in my dorm room, watching *NBC Nightly News* with Tom Brokaw on the 12-inch TV that sat perched atop the mini-fridge. Hundreds of people were standing side-by-side outside an abortion clinic, waving their homemade signs, verbally assaulting the women heading into the clinic. Side to side and up and down, they waved signs that read:

"Baby Killers."
"Abortion Kills."
"Pro-Life & Pro-Child."
"God Save the Children."

Why are these people butting into the lives of people that they don't even know? I wondered. *They have no idea who these women are and what their circumstances are.*

What if someone had been raped and, after that living hell, had gotten pregnant? And then they had to face these jerks? *Don't they understand that no one wants to do this?!* I certainly didn't want to do this. I dreaded it with every fiber of my being. *I am dreading the procedure itself. I am dreading the sadness I will feel, and I am dreading the guilt that I know will plague me for the rest of my life. But I have decided it's best for me and everyone else.*

A balding man with a "Human Rights for the Unborn" sign was being interviewed. "We are working to save lives. Someone has to protect these children," he said emphatically, looking directly into the camera.

The camera panned across the crowd again and then zoomed in on a woman walking in front of them, two companions leading her toward the building. The protesters were shouting, and you could almost see the venom spewing from their lips and landing on her face. Someone threw something at her. The camera zoomed in closer. A doll covered in red paint to look like blood.

I shook my head incredulously. The hair on my arms and neck stood up. I was like a rubber band ready to snap. It made no sense to me at all that these people were more concerned about children that hadn't even been born than the hundreds of millions of children in the world whose lives were horrible. *Why don't they go and take care of the millions of abused or starving children in the world? Haven't they seen the Save the Children commercials?*

My heart began to race. Flames of anger flickered inside me at the injustice of it all, at the unfairness to women.

The anger slowly turned into nervousness and dread, and I began to shake. I pulled the blanket closer around me and curled my arms around my legs, into my body. *I am nervous, so nervous. What if they protest like this at the clinic I am going to? I don't want people yelling at me. I don't want anyone to see me. Why can't they just leave me alone?*

I got up and opened my closet door, pulling back each shirt hanger by hanger in search of my hoodie. I found an oversized black sweatshirt and put it on, pulling the hood up over my head and yanking down on the strings so the shirt was tight against my face. I glanced in the mirror. It covered a good part of my face, but it wasn't enough. *I'll also need a scarf and sunglasses to fully shield myself. I need to be incognito. No one can recognize me.*

A picture from *Our Bodies, Ourselves* popped into my mind, one that will forever be etched there: A naked woman lying face down on the floor, arms out at her sides, palms facing upward, legs folded up under her. A pool of blood surrounds the corpse—dead of a self-induced abortion. The woman jabbed a coat hanger inside herself, ripping apart her insides, and bled to death because she didn't have access to the proper procedure. How desperate and scared she must have been to do this to herself.

We'd talked about this in Women's Studies. How, in the years before Roe v. Wade, the number of self-induced or illegal abortions numbered over one million each year. We'd also talked about how abortion had been a criminal offense. And what made this really insane was that at the same time, giving out birth control information and services was also illegal. Patti, my Women's Studies teacher, had survived a back-alley abortion. She had told us about it just days before this news broadcast.

"I was terrified, of course," she told the thirty-some women and one guy who were in our class. "But I decided after a lot of soul-searching that I just could not have a child with this man I was dating. He was abusive. He was a raging alcoholic. I was afraid of him. So I knew that this was the best option, the best thing for everyone.

"It was scary and dirty and extremely humiliating," she said as she described to us a cross-country journey to Mexico that ended with meeting a connection at a low-budget hotel. "When I think back on it, it's a miracle that I survived. The place was filthy, and I'm sure the instruments weren't even clean, let alone sterile. They blindfolded me before I went into the room, and I had to keep it on the whole time. It was horrible. Just horrible."

A stunned silence filled the room until she continued.

"This is why, ladies—and gentleman—we can't ever take Roe v. Wade for granted. Don't even take birth control for granted. We don't ever want to go back to those dark times."

Dark times, indeed. I glanced back at the television set; the news was now showing a priest at the protest, holding his rosary beads and appearing to pray intently.

The Catholic Church said abortion was wrong. And I could understand that, I guess. But the Catholic Church also said birth control was wrong. And that didn't make any sense at all. Using birth control wasn't a sin; it wasn't wrong. The church was wrong.

The camera panned from the priest to a dozen or so men and women on the other side of the issue. Finally, they were showing us people who were defending the right to choose. The signs on this side read:

"Keep Abortion Legal."

"We Won't Go Back!"

"My Mind. My Body. My Choice."

This sign was the one that resonated the most. I did not want anyone to tell me what to do with my body. I did not want anyone to tell me what to do with my life. It was just so crazy that this political and social firestorm on women's choice happened to be going on right now, right when I had to choose.

These strangers on TV, these people sitting outside abortion clinics all around the country, had no right to harass women who were making one of the most difficult decisions of their lives.

CHAPTER 8

October 11, 1984

I had a dream. The night before my birthday, the night before I was going to have an abortion, I had a dream that seemed so real it shook me to my core.

In my dream, I was at the clinic. With a quivering hand, I signed the necessary paperwork, saying that I understood everything that would happen, that I was ready to do this. A girl who didn't seem much older than me led me back to the procedure room and handed me a paper gown. Feeling this thin, flimsy material between my fingers made me feel even more vulnerable; it could so easily rip apart and be destroyed, just like me.

The girl gave me a comforting smile and gently patted my arm. Then she walked away, leaving me alone in the cold room to get undressed. My shaking grew more intense as I looked at the stirrups on the table. They looked like claws, big claws that were ready to grab me, open me up, rip me apart, and take me down.

I turned so I wouldn't have to look at them and started to undress. Methodically, I took off my jeans, shirt, socks, bra, underwear. I neatly folded them and stacked them one on top of the other on the chair. But then my underwear was lying on top of the pile. I hastily grabbed it and my bra and shoved them to the bottom of the pile so they'd be out of sight. *How stupid, though? Who cares if they see my underwear?* Soon they would be seeing me naked; they'd be looking right inside me.

As instructed, I put on the thin gown and sat in the chair to wait. I clasped my hands, leaned my head down, and prayed. I prayed because there was nothing else left to do. "God, help me through this, and then please forgive me. Please. I will somehow make this up. I will do really good things my whole life and be a good person. I promise. . . . Our Father who art in Heaven, hallowed be thy name . . ."

A tap on the door interrupted my Our Father.

"Are you ready?" the nurse said as she slowly opened the door and stepped over the threshold.

"Yes," I said. But it was a lie. I was not ready. I felt nauseous, and my entire body trembled. I wanted to run somewhere—I didn't know where—but my legs wouldn't work, except to move the few steps to the table. They shook so hard. My whole body shook; I had trouble getting on the table. The nurse guided me over and helped me up.

I felt the needle for the sedative slip easily into my vein, and soon I felt a bit of that ease slide into me. The terror had subsided by a fraction; it was now just extreme fear. I followed directions and put my legs into the stirrups. That's when I began to cry.

"Scooch down a bit," they said. I scooched. "A little more." I scooched again.

"There. That's just right," said the nurse as she sat next to me and held my hand. My other hand lay across my head.

The doctor came in and introduced himself. He asked if I understood what was going to happen.

I nodded. It had been explained to me thoroughly several times.

He took his place at the bottom of the table, and then the noise started. The loud, vacuuming, sucking noise. I closed my eyes and clenched my fists and tried to think of something good, some other place for my mind to take me. But my mind would not let me escape what was happening to my body.

I put my free hand to my face and sobbed, muffling the sound a bit, at least in my head. I felt pain in my vagina and my abdomen. I felt my body jerk back and forth, back and forth with the sound.

Then it was quiet. Eerily quiet.

Dead silence.

I lay there, still, relieved that it was over.

When I opened my eyes and looked around, I was the only one in the room. Everyone had left. And then, just as I began to sit up, the door flew open.

It was my mom.

"Don't look, Mom. Please don't look," I cried. She wasn't supposed to know. Someone must have told her.

I jumped off the table and ran to the canister that had sat at the end of the table. I put my whole body over it so she wouldn't know, so she wouldn't see the blood, see what else was in there. I didn't want her to see what I had done. I didn't want to disappoint her again. We were Catholic; this was a major sin.

Blood was running down my legs, over my feet. It was all over, pooling around me.

"I'm sorry, Mommy. I'm so sorry," I wept as I tried to cover things up. My heart was pounding. I was sobbing, sweating, bleeding.

"I'm sorry, God," I said next. "I'm so sorry. I'm sorry, everyone."

Then, tears running down my face, I opened my eyes.

I felt disoriented; out of place. I glanced over and saw the red light shining on the shelf in my dorm room. The clock read 2:30 a.m.

It was morning, officially my birthday, and I was lying in bed, drenched in sweat and tears. The dream had been so incredibly real that I put my hand down between my legs to check if I was wet with blood. I brought it up again. It was dry. No blood.

It was just a dream. It was just a nightmare.

CHAPTER 9

October 12, 1984

My nineteenth birthday was a glorious fall day, with a bright blue sky and brilliant sunshine. It was one of those days where, on the face of it, the world was perfect.

I stood at my dorm window, looking out at the campus. The grass was still lush and green and the leaves on the oak and maple trees were at the peak of their fall color. They waved to me with brilliant yellow, orange, and red hands. Cool, crisp air seeped in through the open window.

The beauty of what I saw out the window and felt in the air stood in total contrast to what I felt on the inside. Fear, anxiety, sadness, and dread filled up every cell in my body. I was still reeling from the intensity of my nightmare. I felt tense and sick and ready to either explode or collapse.

I caught a glimpse of the US flag across the street flapping in the breeze, and for a brief moment I smiled. It was Columbus Day, when flags are flown and government offices are closed. I remembered what my mom would say to me when I was little: "Well, everyone knows it's your birthday, and those flags are for you." Her words echoed in my head. My mom always did and said special things, things that made us feel like we were the most important people in the world.

But October 12 would never be special again. It would become a day that I'd want to erase from my memory.

I would want to forget this day because soon I would begin my journey to Sioux Falls to meet my friend Jane. She'd made all the arrangements. My appointment was for one o'clock. Afterward, we'd go back to her place so I could recover, and I'd return to Mitchell the next day. And I'd pretend nothing ever happened.

That was the plan, anyway, but I didn't know if I would really be able to do it. Especially after last night's dream.

I turned away from the window and started packing up my things; I grabbed a pair of jeans, a pair of sweatpants, and some comfortable tops and threw them into my bag, right along with my anxiety and fear.

I grabbed the bag and painted a smile on my face. I had to play the part to escape the building. I waved to the girls on the floor as I made my way down the hallway.

"Hey, have a great weekend, Chrisy!"

"Happy birthday!"

"Thanks. You have a good weekend too."

I eased my Ford Futura down the big hill, the trees hugging the road on each side, and then hopped on Highway 169 south. I'd barely reached the outside of the city limits when the big billboard screamed at me from the side of the road:

"Abortion Stops a Beating Heart."

With each mile of my journey, I became more and more nervous. I chain-smoked my Marlboro Lights, one right after another. *At this point, it can't really be a baby. Can it? It's too little. When does life begin, really? And when does it end?*

I hoped they would put me out for all of this so I wouldn't have to think about what I was doing. Because at my core, I didn't want to do it. I would request—no, I would *insist*—that they completely put me under; then I wouldn't have to feel or remember anything. If they put me out, then really, it would be almost like nothing happened. It wouldn't be real. I could only do it if they put me out.

My drive took me through the small towns of central Minnesota. Towns like Lake Crystal, population 2,500, and Windom, 12,000. The further west and south I got from Mankato, the sparser the trees became. Vast fields of wheat and corn spread out across the landscape—you could see forever. If you didn't know the world was round, it was here that you could believe it was flat. The horizon reached on forever.

The "Great Places, Great Faces" sign, with its picture of Mount Rushmore, welcomed me as I crossed the border into South Dakota. Just a few miles after that, another antiabortion sign sat on the side of the road.

I'd noticed them before, of course, but today they taunted me. As if I didn't feel bad enough, I had to look at a homemade, hand-painted sign that screamed: "Abortion is Murder." Again, I wondered why these people didn't put their efforts elsewhere and work to ease the great amount of human suffering in the world—starving and abused children, rape victims. *Why don't they do that rather than make women feel bad?*

Soon I neared the exit into Sioux Falls, South Dakota's largest city despite only having a population of less than a hundred thousand. The entire state contains less than a million people. Sioux Falls, "the big city," was where my mom and Becky and I came each fall and spring to do our big season shopping. It was where the state basketball tournaments were held. It was where the airport was located. It was also where abortions were performed.

I pulled up outside of Jane's small apartment building at eleven. I'd made good time. She must have been waiting for me, because she opened the door just seconds after I knocked. We hugged. It felt so good to be with someone who I didn't have to lie to; someone who knew what I was going through. I didn't have to pretend.

"Happy birthday. Here you go," she said, handing me a jar of pickles. "Your birthday present." I'd always loved and devoured her mom's homemade pickles. I even drank the juice.

"And I've got you something else," she said as she brought out a small, neatly wrapped box. I carefully unwrapped the paper. A Black Hills Gold necklace, which I'm sure she couldn't really afford, lay in the box.

"Thank you. I don't know what I'd do without you. I really don't know." I was deeply touched.

"I also don't know if I can go through with this, Jane. I had the most intense and awful nightmare last night. I think it's a sign." I told her about my dream and let the tears flow as she held me.

As soon as we entered the neighborhood, I could smell the money and the affluence of its inhabitants. I could also sense that we were off course. As Jane maneuvered her car through the streets in this high-end area of Sioux Falls, she began explaining.

"Before we go to your appointment, I thought it would be a good idea to go talk to this lady about your choices and let her help you decide if this is something you really want to do," she said. "Especially after your dream last night. I just want us to be sure."

I shifted in my seat and then turned to look out the window. "Yeah, it'll be good to make sure."

Jane pulled her car into a clean cement driveway in front of a large ranch-style home perched in the center of a perfectly manicured lawn. We barely had time to turn off the car before she appeared—a tall, blonde woman, dressed in slacks and a sweater. She greeted us as soon as we opened the car doors.

"Hi," she said with her big, confident smile and forceful, outreached hand. "I'm Lesley."

Jane accepted her hand. "I'm Jane. I'm the one that called."

"And so you must be Chrisy," she said as she turned toward me and took my hand, firmly shaking it. "We are *so* glad you are here."

My grip was limp and apathetic. Like a dog that could sense fear or danger, I sensed something about Lesley. I was not sure quite what it was, but I knew I didn't really like or trust her.

"Come on in and make yourselves comfortable," she said as she led us into her big, beautiful home. We followed her into the foyer, past the dining room, and into the large family room at the south side of the house. A projection screen sat at one end of the room in front of wall-sized windows that were covered with dark drapes; a film projector took center stage. Two large, comfortable couches came together at a right angle in front of the screen. There was a desk at one end of the room, covered with stacks of paper and brochures. This was no ordinary living room. Jane and I took our seats on the couch, side by side. Lesley sat down next to us, put her elbows on her knees, and folded her hands under her chin.

"I'm glad you're here, Chrisy," she said, acting like she was my best friend. "Jane told me about your situation, and I know how hard it is to face an unplanned pregnancy."

I nodded but said nothing. I felt like I was outside of my body, watching this from above. A surreal experience; I was just an observer. I wanted to get up and run, but my body did not move. Something made me stay.

"My life is dedicated to telling women the truth about their choices, the truth about abortion, and helping them make the right decision," Lesley continued. "You see, most women don't know what they are getting into when they go in for an abortion. So I have a film here that I'd like to show you, so you can see what really happens."

Oh my God. She's one of them. She must be one of those protester types. I wanted to lash out at her and tell her how wrong she was to be cruel to women, but I couldn't move my body or my mouth. It was like I didn't work anymore. Everything just came to a halt.

Lesley got up, closed the curtains, and dimmed the lights. Light flickered onto the screen in front us—a girl appeared. She sat on a picnic table, cradling a young child in her arms. A playground stood in the background; children's laughter filtered in.

"I'm so happy that I decided to have my baby. She is the joy of my life," the girl said. "It's not always easy, but I am so grateful that I have her."

A narrator told us more: Amy had her baby when she was sixteen. She was working on finishing high school and had help from her family caring for her baby.

My mind wandered. I pictured myself in that scene, holding a baby—a cute, blonde-haired, blue-eyed baby—talking about my life as a mom.

Could I really do that? God, I had hardly ever babysat, and when

I did I never liked it that much. I'd never gotten too excited about babies and kids before. I wouldn't know what to do with a baby. But maybe I could do it. Maybe I could be a good mom, with lots of help from my own mom.

Another woman came into focus. She'd had a baby and given it up for adoption. She talked about how hard it was but how good she felt now.

"It's an open adoption," she told us. "So I get to see Riley whenever I want."

We saw her, the adoptive parents, and the baby all together. *That's good, I think, especially for this birth mom. But it must be confusing for the kid.* We'd come a long way—adoption issues used to all be so secretive. But how hard it had to be to see your own flesh and blood and not be the one getting to hold her every day and put her to bed every night.

The story faded into what was meant to be happily-ever-after, and now we heard from a third woman. She'd had an abortion years ago. She regretted it now. She said she regretted it every day of her life.

"I can't look at a child without thinking about it. I am haunted by images of what my child could have been. I am haunted by the sound of the procedure. The sound of a vacuum."

As her voice faded, my heart picked up speed, beating fast and hard in my chest. The narrator explained the abortion procedure as an image of a woman lying on an exam table came into focus. Her legs were in stirrups. Sheets covered her limbs and her crotch. A doctor sat on a chair near her crotch and talked to her, telling her what he was going to do.

The small tube in his hands disappeared under the sheets. The vacuum started.

The girl started crying. Someone was holding her hand. Her body jolted slightly. Blood came out of the tube into a canister.

I heard no more words. My mind spun. My stomach ached. My heart raced. My breathing was heavy; I was going to be sick, to pass out. The tears and anguish I'd been holding back escaped from me in sobs. I knew then, for certain, that I could not go through with the abortion. It was not the right choice for me. It would haunt me my entire life.

Our "hostess" tried to get me to talk, but I didn't want to share myself with this stranger. Jane got my cues and grabbed my hand as we stood to leave.

"It's time for us to go. Thank you," Jane said as she led the way out of the house, Lesley following closely behind.

We didn't talk much driving back to her apartment, mostly because I was crying so much that I couldn't. I cried because I was relieved that I didn't go through the procedure. I cried because now I'd have to tell my parents and family my situation. I cried because I didn't know what the fuck I was going to do now, other than have a baby.

When we got back to Jane's place, we ate pickles and smoked cigarettes. After a while we finally talked about going to the pro-lifer's house. "I took you there because I knew deep down that an abortion wasn't right for you and that you couldn't go through with it. You said you were having serious doubt."

She knew me well, though I wished we would have just talked about it ourselves rather than involving those people—the people who harassed women at abortion clinics, the people who did not support women.

CHAPTER 10

As I drove home to Mitchell, I thought of how much my life had changed in just five months. Five months ago I'd been standing on the floor of the Corn Palace, graduating from high school. Finally, I was moving on to bigger and better adventures.

As we marched into the Palace with our heads held high, I looked up into the nearly full stands, searching for my mom and dad. I found them; our eyes met. I could see the pride and relief on their faces as we smiled and waved to each other.

Hallelujah, they must have been thinking. Their last child was graduating from high school. I'm sure they felt incredibly relieved. I too was relieved and happy. High school had its ups and downs for me, and I was so eager to go to college, to get out of a place where I often felt trapped and bored. I was so excited about going to school and finding a focus, a career path. I was excited about meeting new people and making new friends. I was ready to move out and move on.

We continued marching single-file, in alphabetical order, down the main aisle to take our seats that were lined up on the basketball court. With the last name of Bauer, I was in the front row. I happily settled into my chair to listen to our valedictorians, trying hard not to let my mind wander to the many parties that would take place after the ceremony and the small celebration at home.

Carol was our first speaker. We had gone to Holy Spirit Elementary together way back when, before I left in protest. Carol was always nice, sweet, smart. One of those seemingly perfect kids—homecoming royalty, in the chorus and the school play, honors student—all around good person.

"I am sure we all wish that there were a library where we could look to find all the answers to all of the emotions of life, love, hope, learning, and worry," Carol said.

Her words still resonated with me. I had never thought of Carol as a worrier or someone with trials and errors. But as I turned and glanced at those around me, I supposed we all were to some degree. Maybe high school had been hard for all two hundred of us sitting here, not just me. Maybe we all had many of the same struggles and were more alike than different.

"Since there is no such place," Carol continued, "we just have to learn through trial and error."

These words struck a loud, bold chord as I reflected on my high school years. Yes, I'd spent too much time worrying about other people, and probably too much time partying. I dropped out of most everything for a few years, starting with gymnastics. And I drove my parents crazy, I'm sure.

Then, at the start of senior year, a light bulb went off. I decided it was time to pull it together. After two years off, I went out for gymnastics again. I got focused on school. I took an interest in the present and in my future. I realized I alone controlled my life and my destiny—it was time to get it together. Senior year had been a good year, and I was so looking forward to what the future held.

We clapped loudly as Carol finished her speech and clapped again to welcome Rich, the next speaker. Rich was our class clown, not to mention a National Honor Society member, basketball player, and star of the school plays. His speech was funny, just like him, but also held meaningful messages that resonated with me.

"No matter what you do with your life, make sure that you are happy with what you have and with what you are doing. Live your life to the fullest," Rich said from behind the podium, looking out with his goofy grin at his classmates.

Yes, I said to myself, it was time to live life to the fullest. I was so excited to move on. I was so excited for my future on graduation day.

Now, just five months later, excitement was replaced by fear.

During the hour's drive home from Sioux Falls, I kept repeating to myself my new reality: "I am going to have a baby. I am going to have a baby."

I was finally admitting to myself what I'd known in my heart all along, since I took that very first pregnancy test. I could not pretend it away, I could not ignore it, and while I wholeheartedly believed in my right—and every woman's right—to have an abortion, it was not the right choice for me.

Was it my Catholic upbringing? The values instilled by my family? Or was it that I would regret it and feel guilty the rest of my life? It was likely all those things. This was my fate. I was having a baby.

The trouble was that I myself was still a child in so many ways. I certainly felt that way when I walked through the door of my home.

"You're home early! What a nice surprise," my mom said as she wrapped her arms around me and held me in a deep embrace.

"Hi, Mom. It's good to be home," I sputtered and hugged her back, relishing the safety and security of her embrace and the surroundings of home. "Jane had something come up, so I decided not to stay in Sioux Falls tonight."

Nelly, our black Labrador, and Muffin, our toy Poodle, were quickly at my sides to greet me as well. They nuzzled me and jumped on me, clamoring for my attention. I let go of my mom and knelt down to receive their kisses. "Hi, sweeties. How are you guys? I missed you too! Yes, I missed you. You are so cute, yes you are!" My heart was warmed and my mind relieved for a minute as I played with our dogs.

Oh, how I loved these dogs—and horses, and all animals, for that matter—and I was good with them. Maybe I could be good with a kid.

"And oh, my goodness, happy nineteenth birthday! I can't believe my baby is nineteen!" my mom said so proudly.

I cringed at the thought that her baby was going to have a baby, that I would disappoint my parents, that I'd messed up. I grabbed my suitcase and headed back to my room, Nelly and Muffin following me, their collars and tags clinking with each step.

A tidal wave of relief swept over me as soon as I opened the door to my bedroom. The colors, the shapes, and the smells wrapped around me like a warm wave and engulfed me in solace. I went straight to my bed and lay down. I felt like a baby in a crib—safe, warm, protected. I smiled at Muffin, who stood with her front paws on the bed, waiting for a boost. I lifted her up, put her next to me, and patted the bed with my open hand. "Come on, Nelly, come up!"

Obediently, she jumped up, then quickly lay down as close to me as she could get without lying on top of me. She laid her head on my chest; I stroked her soft, silky black fur and looked into her gentle brown eyes. If I loved these animals this much, I couldn't imagine how much I would love a baby, a baby who grew inside of me and who I would welcome into the world.

I looked around the room. It was a big bedroom—two twin beds, a nightstand, a wicker chair and table, and a large six-drawer dresser with a big mirror. If I took one of the beds out, there would be plenty of room for a crib. And a changing table; I would need a changing table, and a rocking chair. The rocking chair could go in the corner near the window; I could rock the baby there while looking out. That would be peaceful and nice.

This setup would mean that Becky would need to stay on the couch when she came home for visits, but hopefully she wouldn't mind if it was for her niece or nephew. Unlike me, Becky had spent a lot time in her life babysitting. She would make a much better parent than I would. Maybe she could teach me a thing or two about kids.

I looked at Nelly and Muffin again and felt so safe here. I didn't ever want to leave. Just months ago, I couldn't wait to get out of here, out of this house and this town. Now, I couldn't imagine anywhere else I could ever feel this safe.

My mom was what made our home so wonderful. She had dedicated her life to raising us and just when she thought I was heading into a bright future, I was going to drop this bomb on her. *How am I going to tell her?* "Hey, Mom, I'm pregnant." Or, "Mom, I'm knocked up." Or how about, "Mom, your baby is going to have a baby." There was no sequence of words that was quite right.

Even though I was worried about how I would tell my mom this news, I drifted off to sleep. This was nothing compared to the worry I had been feeling before about having to go through with the abortion. It was peaceful to sleep without the blanket of dread and fear that had covered me these past weeks.

CHAPTER 11

Knuckles tapped on my door in staccato rhythm and carried me out of my sweet slumber. I had not slept that peacefully in weeks.

"Hi, honey," my mom said as she cracked open the door and peeked in. Nelly and Muffin wagged their tails in greeting, tap, tap, tapping their smiles on the bed. "Dinner is just about ready, and everyone's here."

"Okay, be out in a minute."

I got myself together and walked into the dining room. My brother Brad was here, as were my brother Curt and sister-in-law DaNette. Here, too, was my father. It was a comfort having everyone here, but I was dreading the conversation to come.

"All right, we can eat now," announced my mom, with a smile that exuded contentment. Her family was together—everyone except Becky, who would be home later. Her children were happy and healthy—or at least appeared to be—three of them gainfully employed, one in college. All was great with the Bauer family, except for me.

We took our seats at the long, elegant dining table. My dad sat at the end that looked out at the living room; my mom faced the mirrored wall. We passed around the beef stroganoff and noodles, the fresh salad and bread. My mom was a wonderful cook, and after a month of dormitory food and pizza, dinner tasted especially good. I loaded up and savored each morsel of this rich, creamy food. I was ravenous and didn't hide it.

"So where is the big party tonight, Chrisy?" Brad asked. "What are your plans for the big nineteen?"

"I don't know what I'm doing yet."

"Big nineteen, little sister," Curt said. "It's party time."

"Yeah, we'll see."

"Something wrong?" Curt asked.

I gulped down the panic that started to make its way up my throat. "Well, I've been doing plenty of that at school. There are parties going on all the time. It's pretty funny; people actually advertise their house parties in the school newspaper."

My dad laughed at that. I glanced to look at him, seeing the family reflected in the mirror. We looked so perfect, like the best family ever. Oh, God, this *was* the best family ever—it was *my* family—but we were not perfect, especially me.

I tried to picture what the dining room table would look like with a highchair pulled up to it. Yes, the baby could sit right there between me and my mom. My mom could help me feed the baby that I pictured as a cute little towhead. She would know what to feed a baby. I didn't know the first thing about what you feed a baby besides a bottle.

"Time for presents!" my mom said enthusiastically, bringing me out of my trance, this temporary fantasy of motherhood. She handed me a large, neatly wrapped box and an envelope.

I opened and read the card. Her sentiments gnawed at me.

"Chrisy, we are so proud of you and so excited for you as you make your way on this wonderful new journey. You will do great things!! We love you, Mom and Dad."

Quickly, I moved onto the package to divert their attention and mine. I tore off the wrapping paper and the popcorn popper box was revealed.

"For the popcorn queen," said my dad. "No one likes popcorn more than you."

"And the great thing is we know it works really good," Curt said. "We tried it the other night. See, there are kernels in there."

I pulled it out of the box and saw the stray kernels. I laughed as I pictured them sitting around eating popcorn.

"You'll get a lot of use out of that at school," Brad assured me. "For when you get the munchies."

Somewhere, I thought. *It will get a lot of use, but I don't know if it will be school.* "All right, let's get things cleaned up and try it."

We cleared the dishes, cleaned up, and then made popcorn. Everyone was shocked that I wasn't going out on my birthday. "I think something's wrong with you!" Curt joked as he and DaNette departed for home. *There is something is wrong with me, and if you only knew,* I thought as I sat next to my mom on our family-room couch. It was just the two of us left; Brad had gone home and my dad had gone to bed.

My mom and I sat side by side in silence for a long time, staring at the television. Every once in a while, we'd make idle chitchat about school and classes. I avoided looking at her, my eyes wandering back and forth from the TV to the coffee table, big nicks and gashes in it from the years of abuse by teenagers. I felt beat up, just like that table. I felt guilty too, wondering why we hadn't taken better care of things for my mom. She was always taking care of us.

Finally, she asked: "Honey, is something wrong? You don't seem like yourself."

Nothing would form on my lips. I couldn't make the words come out and I couldn't keep the tears in. They formed in my eyes and began flowing. My mom immediately put her arms around me and held me tight.

"Oh, honey. What's wrong? What's wrong, sweetheart?" she said with the tenderness of a mother holding a crying newborn.

And then, finally, I said those three words.

"I am pregnant."

With those words, a great sense of relief spilled out of me; the dam had burst. But the relief was intertwined with shame and embarrassment.

"Oh no, honey. Oh my goodness."

"I know. It's the worst thing that could happen to me right now. I just want to die, Mom. How can I be such a fuckup?"

My mom handed me a napkin to wipe the snot off my nose. Nelly got up from her spot on the floor and sat down right in front of me; she put her paw on my knee and laid her head next to that. She sensed my pain, our pain.

"Don't say that about yourself, Chrisy. You are a wonderful person. I am so proud of you."

"I was going to have an abortion today, Mom. That's why I went to Sioux Falls. But I couldn't go through with it. I didn't want you to know." I patted the couch and Nelly jumped up and lay next to me, head in my lap. I didn't tell my mom that I had also seriously considered taking my life, that she could have been planning a funeral instead.

"I feel bad bringing a baby into this world, Mom. I don't think I'd be a good mom. I wasn't even a good babysitter. I love college and I finally feel like I'm where I'm supposed to be."

"Oh, sweetheart, it's going to be hard. But it is going to be okay. You're not alone. I will support you whatever you decide to do. And most importantly, I love you very much. I always love you no matter what."

I dropped this big gigantic bombshell on my mother, and that was her response: that she loved me. Unconditional love. Perfect love. A mother's love.

"I love you too, Mom. And I'm so sorry. I'm sorry I always let you down."

"You don't let me down. You were a challenging and determined teenager, that is for sure, but I love you no matter what and I'm proud of you." And then, after a brief pause, "So what does Jim think? And what do you think you want to do?"

"He supports whatever I want; as far as he knows, right now I've already had an abortion. But I don't know, Mom. I just don't think I can be a parent right now. I love being at college. I know that that is what I'm supposed to do and where I'm supposed to be. Not back in Mitchell with a baby."

"I'm sure you'd be a good mom someday, but it is hard, hard work, Chrisy. And it's forever. Once you start, you can't quit when it gets hard, and believe me, it's hard."

All the trouble I had caused her and my dad over the past few years flashed through my mind: the broken curfews, the partying, the disobedience and disrespect. What a brat I had been when all she had done was be a great mother. She had dedicated her entire life to our family. My dad had dedicated his life to providing for us; my mom was always there at home taking care of us. Putting home-cooked meals on the table every single night, creating a warm and inviting home, washing our clothes, attending our activities, always there for us. Always.

"What do you think I should do?"

I wanted so badly for her to tell me what to do, even though, for all my nineteen years, I'd rarely ever wanted her to tell me what to do. In recent years especially, I got irritated at the slightest suggestion she'd make about anything—school, friends, clothes. Now, I wanted her to tell me what do with the rest of my life and with the life within me.

"I can't make that decision for you, Chrisy. You have to make the decision. And one that is right for you and this baby."

I didn't respond. We were silent for a while. Then she said what kept popping in and out of my mind, like a fly that I kept trying to swat away but just kept buzzing back at me.

"Have you thought about placing the baby for adoption? There are so many good people out there who want to be parents but can't."

Yes, indeed, I had, but it seemed like the hardest choice of all. I knew people who were adopted and who had good lives. A good friend of Curt's was adopted. And one of my dad's employees had adopted a child a few years ago. They seemed fine; they seemed happy. But how were the birth moms doing?

"It would be so hard to have a baby and then give it away to someone."

"It would be very hard, but you'd have lots of support."

The decision seemed to come quickly, but in reality the adoption option had been brewing in my mind since the moment I found out I was pregnant. It seemed like a decision we could live with, but it would be so hard.

CHAPTER 12

Spring 1981
I didn't know it would be this bad. I guess there was a reason you weren't supposed to do things like this when you were barely a high school freshman.

First there was my stomach, which couldn't decide whether it needed to vomit again or if it was hungry. It just kept gnawing at me, incessantly. Then there was my head—it felt like a tiny leprechaun was inside, rhythmically pounding a hammer on my brain. *Bang, bang, bang,* it went, on and on and on. My mouth felt like someone had stuffed cotton balls in it, between my teeth and my gums and underneath my tongue like the dentist does. No matter how much water I drank, I couldn't quench my thirst.

This is how I felt, sprawled out on my bed, when Becky entered my room and confronted me.

"I heard what you did last night, Chrisy. You idiot. You are so stupid," she said. "And I'm telling Mom."

"You don't know anything about what I did last night," I retorted, though from the looks of me plastered onto my bed, it was hard to deny.

"Curt heard from his friends and he told me. And I'm telling Mom. That's just stupid, Chrisy. You're only in ninth grade."

I was indeed only in ninth grade, and I was experiencing a hellacious, atrocious, "I want to die" hangover.

My young body had not just ingested a few beers; my friends and I had drunk cherry sloe gin—nearly a pint each—in what would infamously become known as "Pint Night." In our irrational fifteen-year-old minds, we'd thought, "Let's go for the hard stuff!" since we'd already tried beer here and there. Logistics were worked out so we'd get the goods delivered to us outside of Godfather's Pizza, which was located on North Main Street, just a few blocks from the Corn Palace. Once we got the alcohol, we'd go inside, order pizza, and mix ourselves a few drinks in the bathroom. It was the perfect plan.

"You are such a bitch. I hate you!" I shouted back at my sister, feeling defeated, busted, and sick.

"I hate you, too, you little brat," she said as she stormed out of our bedroom. I'd finally gotten my own bedroom when Becky went away to college, but she was home visiting and clearly getting in my way.

Dread moved into my brain, muscling its way next to the hammering noise. It was going to be bad. Just like last night was bad.

Bits and pieces of the night came back to me. First there was the memory of us getting very loud and obnoxious at Godfather's Pizza. Then leaving there and stumbling over to "The Rec"—short for the Recreation Center, which, ironically, was in the basement of the police station. So much happened right under the cops' noses.

I had faint memories of lying in an alley and throwing up all over the blonde hair that fell to my back; later, of someone hauling me into a shower and getting me cleaned up. I had no idea how we got home to Diane's house, but we woke up there in the morning, both feeling like we'd been run over. I managed to walk the four blocks home and crawl into bed, and I had been immobile since then.

Just as I was pondering why the hell I'd done such a stupid thing, the door flew open. There stood my mom, anger flaring out her nostrils; Becky stood next to her, gloating.

My mom looked at me and shook her head in disgust. She'd been through a lot of shit like this with my oldest brother, Brad, but then Becky and Curt had been pretty much perfect. I had been too until last year, but things were changing for me.

"I hear you're not feeling so good today, Christine Marie. What did you do last night?"

I just stared at her blankly. There's no way I could tell her what I did last night.

"Were you drinking last night?"

I closed my eyes and didn't utter a word.

"If what I'm hearing is true, you are in very big trouble, young lady. I'm asking you again, did you get drunk last night?"

"Yea, I drank a little bit," I answered, knowing that I couldn't deny this one but couldn't give a full disclosure.

"Well you won't be doing that again, because you're grounded for a very long time, young lady. We'll talk about it more when you're in better shape." She slammed the door as she left the room, but Becky stayed; she stared at me in disgust.

"Get out of here," I shouted. "This should be my room now, and you had to come back and ruin it."

"You're an idiot, Chrisy." God, I hated her at that moment. My goody-two-shoes sister, who always did everything right, was getting me in trouble again.

"Well, you're a bitch, Becky, a straitlaced, uptight bitch."

I stayed in bed the rest of the day, too hungover to pretend not to be. I was also ashamed and embarrassed. And I was worried about what my dad would say or do when he found out. I could just say to him, "Well, you do it all the time," but I wouldn't. My dad did drink a lot, sometimes too much, but he never stopped being a good provider, and he reminded us of that.

CHAPTER 13

October 12, 1984

Mom and I were sitting on the couch, letting the reality of it all sink in, when Becky opened the door. Her enthusiastic voice immediately filled the void.

"Hi, girls!" Becky shouted with her usual excitement and energy. She always lit up the room when she walked in. But the look on her face quickly shifted from happy to alarmed when she saw my mom and me huddled together. She could see the despair in our eyes, on our faces, in our slumped posture.

"What's wrong?" she asked.

I waited for a second, hoping that my mom would tell her, but she was leaving it up to me to confess.

"Well, probably the worst thing that could happen to me right now," I said. It was hard to say the words, but again, I pushed them out of my mouth. "I'm pregnant."

Becky looked stunned, like someone has just slapped her across the face. "Oh, Chrisy. Oh, my little sister. I'm sorry." She grabbed me and held me close. The dam of tears burst again—even though I kept trying to repair it, it wouldn't hold. The river of sorrow was flowing rapidly, flooding our home, flooding our lives.

"We'll support you, whatever you want to do," my mom repeated.

"What are you going to do, Chrisy?" Becky asked softly.

I told her what I had planned to do earlier in the day, but that I had eventually aborted the abortion mission.

"I just couldn't go through with it. And now I'm so relieved that I didn't. I don't think that was right, for me, anyway. So now, I'm leaning toward adoption. But how the hell can I do that? How can I trust someone to raise my baby? How would I really know if it's going to a good home?"

My mom moved from sitting next to me on the couch to sitting on the coffee table in front of me. She, Becky, and I now formed a little triangle filled with love and pain. "It would be really hard, honey, but I think it's a good option for you. Someone would love that baby so much. So many people are out there waiting to start a family. You would be doing a wonderful thing, but you'd need Jim's support too."

"What does he think of all this?" Becky asked.

After I told Becky he'd support whatever I wanted, she put her hands on my shoulders to look me directly in the eyes.

"I have an idea, Chrisy. You could come and live with me in Utah. It might be easier to be out where you don't know anyone and don't have to feel like everyone's watching your every move. You'd have time and space to think things through and have the baby out there."

I was taken aback by the offer. After all, we hadn't been the best of friends growing up, and now she was offering to share her one-bedroom apartment with me.

"Wow. That is really nice of you, Beck. That's very kind. Do you really want me to?"

"Yes. I do."

She explained that there was even a college in town, Weber State University. I could keep taking classes and not miss too much school. It would be awful to be pregnant in Mankato with a bunch of partying college kids, and it would be awful to be in Mitchell if I weren't going to keep the baby. Jim might have a hard time with it, and other people just wouldn't understand.

The thought of being far away from everyone and being able to focus on school made the thought of months of pregnancy much more bearable. It was the first glimmer of hope I'd had in weeks. "I can keep doing good things for myself and I'll be doing something good for someone else. I think I want to do this."

Becky's eyes widened. I don't think she was quite ready for me to make up my mind and accept so quickly.

"You don't need to decide right away," she assured me. "You can sleep on it a few days."

"Okay. Thank you so much, Becky. What I don't need to sleep on, though, is having to tell Dad. I just can't tell him or Curt and Brad."

"I will tell them when the time is right," said my mom, "not this weekend."

"Thank you," I sighed in relief. I dreaded the thought of telling my dad and my brothers. It would be too awkward and embarrassing to drop that kind of bombshell on them. I was glad my mom would do this dirty work.

Our conversation came to an end, but Mom, Becky, and I stayed huddled together for a few more minutes. I felt the best I had in weeks. I felt relieved. I felt safe. I was with two amazing women who loved me unconditionally and would be instrumental in helping me do the hardest—and most rewarding—thing I would ever do in my life: become a mother.

CHAPTER 14

October 13, 1984

When I opened my eyes, there she was, just a few feet from me. Becky's face was peaceful and serene as she slept in the bed across from mine. I loved her so much at that moment. For a split second, it felt like a normal day, and I felt like a happy-go-lucky college kid.

And then I remembered. I was a pregnant nineteen-year-old, and today I had to talk to Jim, the father of my child. I needed to tell him what I had decided. That the plans had all changed.

I left the house and steered my car toward Main Street. In Mitchell, people still dragged Main Street—driving up and down from the Sunshine parking lot to First Street and back again. But after moving in that direction, I thought better of it, opting to take side roads and backstreets. I didn't want people to know I was in town. I didn't feel like talking to anyone, but I had to talk to Jim.

I took Havens Street, where I passed my old grade school and the gas station where we used to buy cigarettes at a much-too-young age. We'd still been in junior high. My friend Gretchen used to tell the store clerk they were for her mom; they would look at her skeptically but would sell them to us anyway.

I turned left on Burr, passing another gas station, where I had an unlimited gas account. Anyone in the Bauer family could just pull up and they'd fill it up for us and put it on my dad's bill. He made things easy for us that way, and I don't know if I'd fully appreciated it until now.

After several miles, I reached the road that led to Jim's parents' house, where he lived in the basement. I saw his car as soon as I turned onto the curvy dirt road leading up to the house, and immediately it triggered a rapid heart rate. I reached for a cigarette and felt a very brief sense of relief as I lit up, inhaling that first drag. But just as quickly I felt guilty—smoking was not good for the baby growing inside me. I would have to quit, but I would worry about that later. Not now.

Jim's green car and my yellow one pulled up next to each other, reflective of the autumn scenery around us. It was fitting—we were dying slowly, fading and falling to the ground just like the leaves on the trees around us. With a wave and a concerned smile, Jim got out of his car and came over to greet me. I stepped out of my car and met the embrace of his muscular arms and broad shoulders. "Hey, how ya doin'? Did everything go okay?"

We held each other for a minute, and then I plunged head first into what needed to be said.

"I didn't do it, Jim. I couldn't do it. I told my mom last night, and I decided I'm going to have the baby and give it up for adoption." I took a deep breath and swallowed hard, waiting for his reply.

His eyebrows rose and his eyes widened. He looked surprised and scared. "Why did you change your mind? I thought you didn't want anyone to know. That's what we agreed on."

"I just couldn't do it. I knew deep down it would have bothered me my whole life. It just wasn't right for me. And Jane actually had me go talk to this one lady rather than taking me to the clinic. That was kind of creepy, but I know I couldn't have done it anyway. So I think adoption is the best thing because we can make someone really, really happy. It's been in the back of my mind for a while, and I think it's the right thing."

He held me at arm's length and looked into my eyes, which were brimming with tears just as his were. Gently, he reached up and touched my face, wiping away the tear that was trickling down my cheek.

"Marry me, Chrisy. Will you marry me? Let's get married and keep the baby."

The words flew out of his mouth and hit me. It took more than a few seconds for them to sink in. It wasn't what I'd expected from him, and not how I wanted to be proposed to—not that I'd ever thought about it that much. But certainly not this way.

Searching his deep-set, dark brown eyes, I knew his proposal was based on desperation and fear, not on true love. I could see it in his eyes and on the tension of his handsome, chiseled face. He felt it was his duty to ask me to marry him, like millions of men had done for hundreds of years before in similar circumstances.

And millions of women before me had said yes.

"Oh, you're sweet to ask, but I have to say no. I just can't; we can't. That's not the right thing to do either. We're not ready to be married. At least I'm not ready to be married."

He didn't argue or protest, but he looked defeated and despondent as he crossed his arms and leaned back against my car. We stood in silence for a long while, shoulders touching but both a thousand miles away in thought.

"Yeah, I think you're making a good choice, Chrisy. I think it's the right thing for us and the baby. There are a lot of good people out there who want kids." Jim's sister and brother-in-law were among them. His sister had been trying to have a baby for years, and now, ironically, they just happened to be going through the adoption process.

"Thank you for understanding and being supportive," I said. I shared my plans to go live with Becky in Utah and continue with school, and most importantly to find a good family for our child. In less than twenty-four hours I had made major decisions that would affect me, and many others, every day for the rest of our lives.

Jim and I stood there for a while as the crisp morning air and the musty scent of damp fall leaves settled in around us.

"Let's go do something that makes you happy," Jim said, breaking the silence and pushing himself off the car. "I want to buy you a birthday present. I didn't get you anything yet because I want you to pick it out."

"You don't have to do that. Really, I don't need anything."

"Come on, let's go."

I parked my car in his parent's driveway and got into his. We made our way into downtown Mitchell, passing Mitchell Senior High School. "Home of the Mitchell Kernels," which always made me laugh—a corn cob was our school mascot.

It seemed like a lifetime ago that I was walking the halls of high school, but it had been a mere five months. We passed by the "jock side" parking lot, which butted up to the locker room doors. On the other side of the school, we passed the "burnout side," where the smokers and the burnouts hung out.

I'd never been quite sure where to park because I'd never been quite sure where I fit in. I liked some people from all the cliques—the preps, the burnouts, the jocks. So I took turns parking on both sides, going back and forth depending on the day and on how I felt. Occasionally I even parked on the side street next to the school so I wouldn't have to decide. It was neutral territory; the Geneva of high school parking.

How silly it now seemed that I had felt so suffocated here. Small town life can be comforting and easy and wonderful in so many ways. It was especially so when I was young. My friends and I would ride our bikes downtown, where Woolworth's was one of our favorite spots. It was one of only two stores in town with an escalator, and we'd feel all grown up stepping onto the moving staircase tracks that would take us up to the lingerie section. There we would spend ample time perusing the bras—quietly as we could, we'd go to the dressing rooms to try them on, where our giggles quickly gave us away. Diane was the first amongst us to get a bra—she actually needed one—and I was the last. I finally got it after months of pleading with my mom. She knew my body didn't need one, but my ego sure did.

Woolworth's also had a lunch counter where we could sit on the shiny red vinyl stools and order a Coke or a chocolate shake. It was a good life for a kid. But at some point, the quaintness of my small town began to induce claustrophobia, especially in the past few years. I needed to get out. The world was big and wonderful and I wanted nothing more than to explore it, to meet new and interesting people and see new places. I desperately needed to spread my wings and fly, and I was just getting good air off of the nest when I was shot down.

Jim maneuvered into a parking spot on Main Street, right in front of Woelfle's jewelry store. Holding hands like a happy couple, we walked into the overstocked, family-run store that had been at this location on North Main Street for decades.

Slowly we made our way around the cluttered counter, with Jim periodically pointing out necklaces, rings, and earrings. I paused at the wedding rings, and for a moment—just a brief moment—let my mind indulge in the fairy tale of marriage, complete with a handsome prince, a long white dress, and a beautiful ring. But a fairy tale was a tale, after all, and as we'd talked about so many times in Women's Studies class, in real life there was no guarantee for happily ever after.

I was startled out of my daydream when Jim approached me with a pearl necklace. He held it in his strong, rough hands, rubbing the small white beads between his fingertips.

"Do you like this? I heard that every girl needs pearls."

I smiled at him and his thoughtfulness. "Yes, I do. I like it." It was beautiful, symmetrical, perfectly formed. It was so unlike me.

CHAPTER 15

October 15, 1984

My weekend at home came to an end. It was time to go back to school, where I had to pretend again.

"Hey, how was your weekend? Did you have a great birthday?" I hadn't even reached my dorm room before being peppered with questions from Kim, my next-door neighbor. She walked toward me down the hallway and stopped in front of my door as I juggled bags in my hand to find the keys.

"It was just really nice to be home," I told her.

I had just left four hours ago and already desperately wanted to go back to the shelter of home, to the love of my mother's arms. I'd left without telling my dad or my brothers the news. We agreed it would be best for my mom to tell them, mostly because I didn't want to see the hurt and disappointment in my dad's eyes and the awkwardness from my brothers.

"Did you go out and celebrate like crazy? Was it fun seeing Jim?"

"Yes, it was nice," I said, and thought how she would flip if I told her he proposed to me this weekend.

"Well, Cam and I got in a huge fight again this weekend. Oh my God, it was so bad and it was so stupid."

I nodded my head in agreement, thinking, *He is stupid, this is stupid, and I want to care but I don't care at all.* I was pregnant and I was tired; this was so insignificant for me. I unlocked my door, opened it, and picked up my bags to step inside.

"Can I come in? I'll tell you about it over a smoke," Kim said.

"Sure," I responded automatically, not wanting to be rude. I put my bags down and she followed me in, holding her Marlboro Reds and her Bud Light.

"Do you want a beer? I'll go grab you one," she said as she loudly exhaled after lighting her smoke.

"Nah, no thanks. I had enough over the weekend."

I sat comfortably in the large beanbag chair on the floor of my room and listened to the story of the fight, the drama, and the makeup. God, I wished my troubles were so easy.

"Thanks so much for listening and for caring," Kim said as she got up to leave, giving me a quick hug. "You're the best."

From that day on, I got really good at listening—or at least appearing as though I were. It meant that I didn't have to talk much about myself. What would I say? "I know you are stressed over finding the right clothes for the party, but I'm stressed about finding a family for my baby."

My life was no longer anything like my friends'. I was not a carefree college kid, looking for the next party or a cute guy, wondering what to wear and where to get the best and cheapest pizza. I was growing another life inside me and trying to get good grades. That was my focus. I just needed to make it through the next two months without telling anyone that I was going to have a baby.

CHAPTER 16

November 1984

In Women's Studies we were reading *The Yellow Wallpaper and Other Writings*, a book of essays and short stories by Charlotte Perkins Gilman. Gilman was ahead of her time. She was a pioneering feminist and activist, and as I read her work, I knew that if I had lived during that same time—1860 to 1935—I would have been just like her or at least wanted to be like her, protesting and speaking out on the importance of women's rights and economic independence.

It was the exact opposite of what the protestors today were doing—at least the protestors who were getting all the attention. The ones outside the abortion clinics fought against women's rights, against economic freedom, against women's control over their bodies. That was why I hated them.

It's hard to imagine living back then, having no rights. None. For many centuries, women belonged to their husbands; they were property of their husbands or male relatives. Women had no right to vote. No control over their bodies. They could not own property, so even if their husbands died, it went to someone else. They couldn't use their talents for a career. About the only thing women could do was get married, and that's when they lost their names and identities. I asked my mom about the name thing on one of our phone calls:

"Why do your checks and all your things say "Mrs. James Bauer"? That gives you no identity, Mom, only Dad's identity. You are Donna Bauer. Not James Bauer."

"Well, I don't really know," she said. "I guess that's just what everyone does, or at least that's what everyone did."

I wasn't going to change my name when I got married. Why shouldn't the man have to change his?

For so much of history—most of it, really—being born a woman meant that you kept quiet, got married, and had babies. Oftentimes, lots of babies. I would have gone crazy—really, really crazy—if my life would have been controlled and suffocated like that. Many women did, like the narrator of "The Yellow Wallpaper." The character suffers from severe postpartum depression, like Charlotte Gilman herself, who fell into deep depression after the birth of her first and only child.

If a physician of high standing, and one's own husband, assures friends and relatives that there is really nothing the matter with one but temporary nervous depression—a slight hysterical tendency—what is one to do? Gilman wrote. *I am absolutely forbidden to "work" until I am well again.*

They would not let her do what she loved, which was writing. She was supposed to do nothing. Just lie in bed and go crazy.

I felt like I was going crazy sometimes, being pregnant and telling no one. Was there such a thing as pre-partum depression, I wondered? On many days, it was hard to even get out of bed. It was hard to eat. It was hard to sleep. It was hard for me to sit through my classes without shouting out "I'm pregnant," especially in Women's Studies, where everything we talked about in some way touched me directly—discussions on birth control, the right to choose, equal protection under the law. The list went on and on.

At the same time, it was comforting to be sitting in that class, learning about how powerful I was in so many ways, about the reinforcement that came with my right to choose. *I am choosing to have a baby.* I came so close several times to revealing my secret, but I didn't want to call attention to myself. I wanted to blend in with the wallpaper.

You think you have mastered it, Gilman wrote, *but just as you get well underway in following it, it turns a back-somersault and there you are. It slaps you in the face, it knocks you down, and tramples upon you. It is like a bad dream.*

This pregnancy and depression had slapped me in the face, knocked me down, and trampled upon me. It was hard to get up. It was like a bad dream.

I don't know if I can I handle it, I thought. *Can I grow this baby inside me and then give it away to someone else? Can I give my flesh and blood away to someone I don't even know? What if they are mean to my baby? What if she has a shitty life, and life with me would have been better? What if she gets sick and dies and I never get to know her? What if I get sick and die and she can never meet me?*

What if I get postpartum depression like the woman in "The Yellow Wallpaper"? It's quite possible that I could get stuck lying in a bedroom, just staring at the walls as they—and the whole world—close in on me.

CHAPTER 17

November–December 1984

If postpartum depression was worse than what I was going through during pregnancy, I didn't know if I could survive it. In the early months, I cried every single day, sometimes many times. I cried for this baby inside me. I cried for myself and for Jim. I cried for my parents.

"What's wrong, Chrisy? How come you're crying?" Judi, my roommate, climbed down out of her bed, stepping across the counter and onto the ladder that leaned against my bed. Her head was even with mine, which was turned toward the wall.

"I've heard you crying before, and I'm really worried about you," Judi said as she gently put her hand on my back. "You can tell me what's wrong. Maybe I can help."

I took in a deep breath and then let it out, slowly, deliberately, as I stared at the wall just a foot from my face. "Thanks, Judi, but there's nothing you can do. I'm pregnant. I'm leaving school because I'm going to have a baby, not because I want to try another school like I told you earlier. I'm going to have a baby and give it up for adoption."

She touched the back of my head. "Oh, I'm so sorry. I could tell something was going on. You should've said something before. I would have helped or at least listened. That's a very brave thing you are going to do," she said softly, the utmost compassion in her voice.

"Oh, Judi, I don't know. I don't know if it's brave or if it's a cop-out. But thank you for being supportive. I really appreciate that."

When I finally fell asleep that night, I slept well. I was relieved that I wouldn't have to be secretive with everyone anymore. Judi and Robin, who I'd tell in the morning, would know that there was a reason I felt like sleeping at all times of the day; there was a reason

I wasn't excited about going to parties anymore; there was a reason I wasn't drinking beer anymore. There was a reason for everything.

"Wow, that's huge news. Oh my God!" exclaimed Robin. We were sitting on the floor of my room, drinking coffee and smoking cigarettes. "This freaks me out! This happened even though you were using the Today Sponge? Do you know how many times I've done it without using anything? Tons of times! My high school boyfriend and I screwed like rabbits and only used the withdrawal method. Holy shit! I should be the one that's pregnant."

We laughed at that for a moment.

"So I just want this to stay with the three of us, okay? My plan is to go to Utah and live with my sister until the baby is born. I'm going to take a few classes there, and then I'm going to come back here in the fall."

"Yes, you have to come back here. You have to." Robin leaned over and gave me a hug.

"I want to come back here and have it be just like it is now," I said.

"It will. And one other thing: you have to quit smoking," Robin said.

"Yeah, I know. I know. But at least I'm not drinking. And I have cut back a little bit. I'm just too stressed to quit now. I have to make it through the semester." I still had a couple of months to go before final exams and then I could get out of here.

Robin and Judi kept my secret, and with their help and an incredible amount of determination, I made it through my first semester of college, ending up with a 3.0 grade point average. Then it was time to leave; time to bid my sad goodbyes to these wonderful friends I'd made in just three short months.

"I promise I'll stay in touch," Judi said as she gave me a hearty embrace. "I'll write to you and call you a lot and before you know it you'll be back here."

"I promise I'll be back next fall," I pledged. "Really, I'm coming back no matter what!"

"Good luck with everything," Robin said. "I'll be thinking about you a lot."

Judi and Robin left, as did the others on the floor, and soon it was eerily quiet. From my dorm room window, I watched the snow gently fall on the quiet, still campus. It looked so serene out there, barely a car in sight. Inside it was nearly as quiet. The air was devoid of the usual dorm floor sounds—no music blaring through the doorways, no televisions humming, no laughter or chatter bouncing off the walls. Just me with boxes to pack and deafening silence.

My mom would be here in the morning, so it was time to start packing. I grabbed my desk lamp, winding the cord around and around the base and setting it in the box. Next, I took the picture frame that held the photograph of my dad and Nelly staring into the fireplace, freezing a beautiful moment in time. I packed it away and grabbed the next item—the four-by-six brass frame that held the photo of me and Jim, taken outside the church where Curt and DaNette's wedding rehearsal had taken place just months earlier. I held it with both hands and pulled it close to my face to examine it.

I was dressed in a silk, blue-and-grey dress with open-toe grey pumps. Jim was in a dark-brown suit with a striped tie. We were standing in front of the church, holding hands and smiling. Our faces—mine framed with sun-streaked blonde hair and his outlined with thick, jet-black hair—were beaming with carefree, fun-loving smiles.

The photo had been taken only five months ago, yet it seemed like a lifetime. So much had changed. With my index finger, I touched Jim's face before wrapping the frame in newspaper and putting it in the box. It was time to tuck us away.

I continued packing the surface and contents of my desk, thinking of how much I'd used my dictionary and thesaurus the past few months. I was proud that I'd ended up with a decent grade point average, considering the stress I was under and the incredible, knock-me-on-my-ass fatigue. I did it because I'd needed to prove to myself that I could do anything, that I was strong.

Slowly but surely, I packed up all of my belongings. And slowly but surely, I also packed my insecurities, my fears, my doubts, and my sadness about what I was leaving and what lay ahead. I put them right in there next to everything else I'd be carrying out tomorrow.

CHAPTER 18

December 24, 1984

I'd been home from school for three weeks and had barely left the house during that time. I didn't want to see or talk to anyone. I wanted as few people as possible to know about what was going on with me. I hated being the center of gossip, a hallmark of small towns. I didn't see Jim that much either; I didn't want him to change my mind. I didn't want him to convince me to stay or to get married. I'd made up my mind.

I lay very low in my time at home, though I would be making an outing later this day. It was Christmas Eve, and my brother Brad and I were sitting in the living room, where a fire crackled and popped in the fireplace. I was waiting for my dad to get home. I looked at the grandfather clock that stood stately against the wall—quarter to two. The stores would close at three.

"He'd better get home soon," I said to Brad, breaking the silence.

"He'll be here just in time, I'm sure," Brad said. "Unless, of course, he decided to play Santa."

We both laughed out loud at this, remembering the many Christmas Eves through the years that my dad took it upon himself to spread holiday cheer by donning a cheap Santa suit and beard and stopping by the homes of friends and employees to play Santa Claus. He'd make his way around town, spreading the Christmas spirit with a jolly "ho, ho, ho" and pulling a good bottle of Scotch out of his gift sack. Santa's generosity was much appreciated and, of course, reciprocated with a drink before he headed back out into the cold.

We could always tell if Santa had covered a lot of territory—he'd be late and suffering the effects of a few too many. He'd come in from the cold and peel off the layers of his Santa suit, hot, sweaty, and red in the face. I was always worried he'd keel over from a heart attack, but he always managed to defy the odds and pour another drink, light up a smoke, and tell us about his adventures.

I listened to the grandfather clock *tick, tick, tick* and then chime when it struck two. Finally, I heard my dad come in. I jumped up from my chair and went into the kitchen to greet him.

"Come on, Chrisser. Let's go," he said as soon as he saw me.

My mom, already hard at work preparing Christmas dinner, knew that we are going at the very last minute to get her Christmas present, as we'd done many Christmases before. "We'll be back soon," I said as I gave her a quick kiss on the cheek.

"Yes, you will, since the stores close in an hour," she said.

I grabbed my coat. My dad and I headed outside and slid into each side of his emerald-green Lincoln Continental. "I was getting a little worried there, Dad," I said as soon as we were settled into the still-warm car.

"Oh, we've got plenty of time," he assured me as he turned the car toward downtown and Dahle's Jewelry, where they were probably expecting us.

After those first few words, an awkward silence sat in the space between us in my dad's big, boxy car. My dad and I had not been alone like this since I came home, and we had not yet talked much about me and the baby.

My mom had been the informer and the go-between for me and my dad on my situation, as she had been for so many other things over the years. And now, here we were, traveling down the snow-covered roads, just the two of us. It was finally time to talk about it. We could no longer avoid it.

"So how are you doing, sweetheart?" he asked. "Are you doing okay with everything?"

The words formed right away on my lips but did not come out entirely truthfully. "I'm all right, Dad."

Sometimes there was an awkwardness between my dad and me, at least these last few years. Perhaps it had to do with him seeing his baby girl grow up into a rebellious and challenging teenager. Perhaps it was that we really didn't spend much time together anymore. He always worked a lot, but when I was younger, he made time to be in a father-daughter program with me and always attended my gymnastic meets. He also let me tag along sometimes with him and my brothers when they went fishing and trap shooting, but the older I got, the further apart we grew.

"I know this is hard on you, and it's really hard on your mom. But it's going to be okay."

And it's hard on you, Dad, I thought but didn't say. I knew it was hard for him to know his little girl was going to have a baby. Maybe I felt most awkward about my situation with my dad because I always wanted and needed his approval, and surely I was letting him down.

"I'm really sorry, Dad. I'm always screwing things up, aren't I?"

"We all make mistakes, Chrisy. That's life. God knows, I've made lots and lots of mistakes in my life. But you make the most of it and you move on."

Main Street was pretty much deserted, so there were plenty of parking spaces along the street. We pulled into a parking spot right in front of the store and sat for a minute with the car still running, the heat blaring at us.

"What you are doing is really hard, Chrisy, but I think you are making the right decision. Raising kids is hard work; even though you're nineteen and feel grown up, you're still a kid."

I smiled, nodding ever so slightly. Yes, as much as I had spent the past several years rebelling against my parents and authority in general, wanting to leave home and be free, I was still just a kid.

"I know. I'm not ready to be a mom. I really want to finish school and get a good job. There's so much I want to do."

"You'll do them, sweetie. You're a smart kid, a good kid. You'll do lots of great things." He put his hand on mine, squeezed it, and leaned over to give me a sweet peck on the cheek.

Although the gesture was small and the words were few, they made a big impact because they came from my dad.

CHAPTER 19

December 25, 1984

The room was dark except for the lights on the Christmas tree as I quietly stepped into the soft glow at this predawn hour. It was magical, peaceful.

I repositioned the chair so that it directly faced the tree and then sat down to admire it. Our nine-foot Douglas fir stood proudly in the room, in the same spot our tree stood every one of the fifteen years we'd lived in this house. The tree had its traditional white flocking, which along with the red lights wrapped around the branches gave it a soft red radiance. Hundreds of ornaments, each with some story or meaning, completed our glorious tree. Some of the ornaments were made by my mom when she and my dad were first married. I think it was partly out of necessity (they didn't have much money) and to serve as a creative outlet for my mom. Some of the ornaments came from my parents' travels to far reaches of the world. Others had unknown origins; they'd been hanging on the tree every year of my life. There was a strange and wonderful comfort and stability in that simple thing.

I used this quiet time to reflect on my appreciation for my mom and dad for always making Christmas so special. I was so blessed to have such a loving family. *God, I am so lucky. Thank you, God, and happy birthday, Jesus.* These sights and sounds of Christmas were so consoling. I drew in a deep breath and savored the scent of fresh pine emanating from the tree and mingling with the smell of the cinnamon-scented candles that were tucked in between the fresh garland on the fireplace mantel.

I hadn't been in the Christmas spirit much this year, but I was starting to feel it now. And for a moment, I was starting to forget the adult decisions I faced and feeling like a bit of a kid again. The presents under the tree and gifts bulging out of the stockings suddenly became tempting. Christmas morning was always fun and this year didn't have to be different, but I had to wait for everyone else to wake up before opening any gifts.

I decided to put the temptation out of sight by moving into the family room to watch TV until the rest of the family woke up, but I quickly found out that was a mistake. With a click of the remote control button, the peace and serenity of my morning were shattered.

On the TV screen just feet in front of me, reporters and camera crews were swarming outside a smoldering building in Pensacola, Florida. An abortion clinic and two physicians' offices had been bombed in the early morning hours by a group of antiabortion protesters. The perpetrators were two twenty-one-year-old men and two eighteen-year-old women. They were calling the bombings "a gift to Jesus on his birthday."

I stared at the TV. *Help me, Lord. I just can't make sense of the world.*

Shock from the bombing news quickly morphed into anger as the reporters and anchors continued to spout out information about antiabortion violence. At least two dozen clinics had been bombed this year alone; hundreds of acts of vandalism had occurred; abortion providers had been assaulted. It all added up to women being continually threatened and assaulted for their right to choose what to do with their own bodies and lives.

I thought back to the pro-lifers I had met and talked to. I should have told them that I thought what they did at the clinics was wrong. It was wrong to harass and abuse women and clinic providers. It's one thing to provide information, and it's quite another to assault someone you know nothing about. You are not—and never will be—in her shoes.

Those Three Words

The Christmas dinner did not smell good. The scent of the hospital-cooked turkey and potatoes and gravy that filled the air in my mom's Ford Tempo made me nauseous. My breakfast was making its way up my throat. I was going to be sick. "Mom, you need to pull over. Now," I said.

I threw open the door as she steered the car to the side of the road next to the waist-high snowdrift. I leaned out the side door and took in the fresh, cold morning air. I didn't get sick after all.

It was late Christmas morning and my mom and I were out driving the streets of Mitchell, delivering Meals on Wheels to elderly people who lived alone. My mom had delivered meals every week for as long as I can remember. We kids went with her once in a while when we were young, but it dwindled off as we got older and thought we were too cool to do things like that. I was happy to be delivering again this morning; spreading a little joy would help me mask my sorrow.

"All right. Where to next?" my mom asked as she pulled back onto the street, white and glistening with fresh-fallen snow. I read the name and address to her, and within a few minutes we pulled up in front of a tiny, run-down house on East Second Street. The house needed painting, and the sidewalk and driveway were packed with snow as a result of lazy shoveling.

We got out of the car and pulled the containers from the back. The smell of this hospital food was bad on any given day, but being four months pregnant made it even worse. My mom grabbed the hot meal in the styrofoam container and I grabbed the cold milk from my side. Together we stepped carefully up the sidewalk to the front door and rang the bell.

The door flung wide open immediately; the homeowner had been waiting for us. We were likely the only faces she would see that day.

"Merry Christmas!" said the tiny, elderly woman, donning her housedress and slippers. As she smiled, I saw big gaps where some of her teeth were missing. She brushed back her greasy, thin hair and gestured for us to come into her living room. "Come in, come in. Please sit down." The invitation bordered on pleading.

"Of course, we'll come in, but it'll just be for a few minutes," my mom told her as she gently patted the woman's arm. "We got a few more stops to make this morning." The lady took the meal we had brought for her, set it on the TV stand in front of her frayed, faded lounge chair, and sat down. My mom and I sat on the sofa across from her, her loneliness drifting our way. I watched and listened as my mom leaned forward and interacted with this old, frail woman who was alone not just today, I guessed, but most every day.

She smiled and became animated as she talked to my mom, someone who cared. Even though it was just for a few minutes, we had made an impact on this woman's day through a small act of kindness. My mom was always doing that.

We stayed more than a few minutes. It was hard to leave. "I'll stay longer next time," my mom assured the old woman, leaning down to give her a hug.

"Thanks for coming. I hope you have a good Christmas. And it was so nice to meet you, Chrisy."

"Merry Christmas to you, too," I said and turned to hug her.

"Isn't she sweet?" my mom said walking back to the car.

"It's so sad that these old people are all alone on Christmas; they don't have any family," I said. "I'm glad we can help a little." My mom turned and smiled at me and patted my arm. "Where to next?"

As we drove through the peaceful, snowy streets, the importance of family resonated with me even more. My family was a good one, and my baby would be missing out.

CHAPTER 20

January 1, 1985
"Jesus, Chrisy, you're going to be a big heifer if you keep eating like that."

The words came buzzing out of nowhere and stung like a bee. Quick and sharp, and the stinger remained after impact.

I turned toward my dad, shocked.

"I haven't eaten that much!" I said defensively, glancing down at the bowl in my hand. The homemade trail mix of cereal, pretzels, and nuts was so salty and good, but I didn't want it anymore. I finished the handful that I was eating and then got up to throw the rest away.

Even though it hurt, I knew my dad's comment had nothing to do with me getting "fat" but everything to do with the fact that he was having a hard time watching his little girl—his princess—transform from a young lady into a pregnant woman. My mind flashed back to the earlier, much easier days when I would sit on his lap right there on the chair in the kitchen and enjoy his hugs. He'd call me his little princess and tease me that I needed to sit on his lap and hug him every day, because one day I wouldn't do that anymore. I'd always say, "Oh, Daddy, I'll always sit in your lap."

But, of course, he was right. At some point, I quit sitting in his lap and we quit hugging. Those tender moments we shared were long gone.

As hard as it was for him to watch me transform from a nineteen-year-old college kid into a pregnant woman, it was even harder for me to do it. I wanted to be thinking about what subjects to take at school and what career I might have rather than the fact that I was growing another life inside me.

Although I had made a pact with myself that I wouldn't gain more than twenty pounds the entire pregnancy, the weight was slowly creeping on; ounce by little ounce it was clinging to me and wouldn't let go. It was frustrating not being able to control what was going on with my body. For most of my life I'd been very conscious of my weight, much of which stemmed from being a gymnast and some of which came simply from being a teenage girl. Now, I had no control. There was simply nothing I could do. It was like my body was a house and a robber had broken in; I was being ransacked over and over again, and each day the robber was leaving behind a great big mess.

My dad watched as I emptied the bowl and put it in the dishwasher. Our eyes met again, and I knew he felt bad the minute the words had left his mouth. But he couldn't take them back. The stinger was still there, the damage done.

"I guess I'll go pack now," I said as I passed him and went back to my bedroom. Even though I was packing for a five-month stay, it would not take long. It doesn't take long when you don't have many clothes that fit.

CHAPTER 21

January 2, 1985

I would be gone for nearly five months, but I only had two suitcases to check. I would be borrowing or buying new clothes to fit my changing body.

Brad and my dad carried our luggage from the Suburban into the one and only terminal at the Sioux Falls airport, where Becky and I would catch our flight to Salt Lake City. As we made our way through the small airport, the impact of what I was doing became more intense. My chest got heavy and my stomach was in knots. Every fiber in my body was tensing up, trembling.

I'd had anxiety attacks on and off during high school; now another one was lurking just around the corner, waiting for the right moment to jump out. I worked hard to keep it at bay by taking deep breaths and repeatedly telling myself that I didn't want to make this any worse for my parents than it already was.

When we arrived at the gate, we stood still and quiet for a while. I looked at my family, heavy winter coats tucked under their arms, and could see the fear in all of their faces. We were all scared as hell, but we did not say it or talk about it. We were all wondering if this was really the right thing to do. *Should I be staying here in South Dakota and welcoming a new member into the family?*

We were surrounded by other families gathered at the airport, but those families were smiling, laughing, hugging. Their arms were loaded down with bags that looked like they contained new and fun Christmas items. Surely, they were simply sending someone back home after the holidays; clearly none were sending the youngest child off to another state to have a baby.

We all stared out the window for a few minutes, watching the airport ground crew working in the ten-below-zero temperature. It was even colder than that with the wind chill factored in, part of life in South Dakota. With few trees to break the wind or block the sun across the flat, barren prairie, our weather was extreme. Temperatures in South Dakota range from fifty below zero in the winter months to well over a hundred degrees in the summer. When it was extremely hot or cold, I always thought of my mom and her family, who lived in a one-room wooden house—a shack, really—in the middle of the prairie, with no running water and no electricity. It was amazing they survived. I admired my strong, hearty people.

The workers' warm breath mixed with the frigid air and created a fog around their heads. They moved swiftly and intentionally, grabbing bags and throwing them into the plane's underbelly. I watched as my two suitcases were heaved onto the plane.

Becky broke the silence and tension by proclaiming: "It was a great Christmas, once again! Thanks, Mom and Dad." She could always be counted on for striking up and stoking the fire of conversation. Becky had a gift for that.

Our flight began boarding soon after we arrived at the gate, which was good because I didn't want to linger; if I thought about it too much, I might turn around and run. I wanted to run faster and harder and longer than I ever had, away from this decision, from my life, from the pain I was causing everyone. I wanted to run away from it all.

Instead, I turned to my mom and hugged her. "I love you, sweetheart," she whispered into my ear. "It's going to be okay." Her words were soft and soothing, but her embrace was strong and determined. I knew it must be hard for her to be sending her baby and her baby's baby away on the next airplane.

I didn't say anything because I was afraid to open my mouth, afraid of what would come out. Instead I moved from her to my dad; his embrace was just as strong and loving, but I could feel the uncertainty and fear in his sturdy chest. "I love you, sweetie," he mustered.

By the time Brad and I hugged, the tears were seeping from the corners of my eyes, but I managed to suppress the sobs, taking long, deep breaths through my nose. Over and over, I told myself, *Hold it in; don't cry.*

I let go then and headed toward the ticket agent and the walkway, suppressing the urge to look back at my family. I wanted to look back but I didn't. I couldn't. I could only look forward.

Becky caught up with me, and we walked side by side down the entryway to the plane. Then, slowly, gently, she reached over and took hold of my hand.

CHAPTER 22

Mid-January 1985

I was a fish out of water, the elephant in the room. I was a pregnant, teenage Catholic living in the land of Mormons.

All around me were married, pregnant women waiting to be seen by Dr. Hunter, the man who would bring my baby into the world. I was referred to Dr. Hunter by a friend of Becky's; he was supposed to be the best ob-gyn in Ogden, and he also set up open adoptions. So, there I was, waiting to see the good doctor.

The small waiting room was cramped with uncomfortable women perched on comfortable couches. My discomfort, though, weighed more on the mental than the physical side. My psyche was racked with guilt and sorrow. *I should be excited to have a baby and to be a mom like these women are, but I'm not.* I was just sad as I listened to them talk.

"Oh, I've been craving potato chips and chocolate like crazy," said one woman. "What a weird and unhealthy combination." Others chimed in about their different cravings—pickles, ice cream, Taco Bell.

Unfortunately, my craving came to mind: nicotine. God, I would've loved a cigarette right then. I was dying for one. It would calm my nerves and comfort me like an old, familiar friend. I hadn't had one in weeks, and I wanted one so badly. But I'd promised Becky and the baby that I would quit.

I looked at the women around me and laughed to myself, wondering what they would think if I shouted that out: "You know what I'm craving, ladies? I'm craving a cigarette."

They would be appalled by all of it—that I was pregnant, that I liked cigarettes, *and* I liked beer. Mormons—and not just the pregnant ones—aren't supposed to smoke or drink alcohol or caffeine. And they most certainly don't give their babies up for adoption.

I watched as the women happily patted their bulging stomachs and stretched their aching legs. I decided then and there I would not tell anyone at my new school or any of the women in the doctor's waiting room about my baby and my plan. How could any of them possibly understand? A Mormon woman's greatest career is motherhood. To them, I would be an anomaly, a freak.

I listened to the chatter as I pretended to read *Parents* magazine. "This is number six for me," said one woman, who only looked to be in her early thirties.

"Congratulations," chimed several other women. "This is just my second one," said one, "but they are close together. My first one is just six months old."

"I know what it's like having them close together," said the mom of six, who looked exhausted and half asleep.

I tried to shut them out then because I didn't want to hear or share their happiness. I was just so different from them. They were married. I was single. They were in their twenties and thirties; I had just turned nineteen. They were happy and excited to be expecting babies. I was sad and terrified of my pregnancy. They were thinking about how fun it would be to bring their newborns home. I was agonizing over the thought of handing my newborn over to strangers.

I redirected my thoughts and instead tried to focus on the magazine in my hands. I scanned the articles: "Taking Care of Baby's Skin." "Toddler Danger Zones." "Making Room for Baby—Decorating Ideas." But I couldn't read any of them. They didn't apply to me. I wondered, though, if my baby's future mother had read any of this stuff. *I hope so. She needs to know this. Even though I don't even know who she is yet.*

Whoever you are, lady, please keep my baby safe, and healthy, and happy. Please. I hoped she was listening.

Finally, after half an hour, my name was called. Dutifully, I followed the nurse; it was time to share my list with Dr. Hunter, the list he asked me to put together on my first visit here.

Dr. Hunter was going to help me find a family for my baby. It would be an open adoption—that was the only way I would do it—because I didn't want any secrecy or sealed records. I wanted to know who the parents were, their names, where they lived, what they did for a living, what they did for fun, what they believed in, what they cared about. I wanted to be able to contact them and them me if needed. I wanted to know where my baby was going so that I could always find him or her.

Dr. Hunter was seated behind a big mahogany desk in his office, cluttered with photos of dozens of smiling children. "Have a seat. Make yourself comfortable," he said with a smile, clearly trying to make me feel at ease. He got up and made his way around the desk, taking the chair next to mine. I clutched the piece of paper—the list—in my hand. "It looks like you did your assignment," he said. "Did you spend a lot of time thinking about this?"

"Yes, I did. Lots of time," I said, leaning toward him and handing him the piece of paper, which listed my criteria for parents. My hands were shaking, and I felt sick. Handing him this list seemed so insensitive and awkward. It felt like it was an order form—like I was ordering a pizza and these were my must-have toppings.

Dr. Hunter moved his gaze from me to the list that was now in his hands. I watched him as his eyes scanned the list.

At number one, I had written: non-Mormon. (No anchovies, please.) It's not that I didn't think a Mormon family could be good parents. Rather, I didn't understand or feel comfortable with a religion that told you no to alcohol, tobacco, and even caffeine. Why would God care if you enjoyed those things? Then there was "Mormon underwear" they had to wear; I didn't get that either. I also didn't want my kid traipsing across the country in black pants, white shirt, and black tie, doing door-to-door evangelizing. And what really bothered me was that women were seen as baby-making machines.

"No offense to you, Dr. Hunter," I said. "But I want to stick with what I'm familiar with, Catholic or Lutheran or even just spiritual." Of course, the Catholic church also treated women like shit with their stance on birth control and not letting them be priests, but at least I was familiar with that territory.

A smile passed his lips quickly. "No problem. No offense taken." His eyes scanned the rest of the list:

- Strong ties with their families. Grandmas and grandpas, aunts and uncles, and cousins are a fun and important part of growing up.
- Stable couple. Married for at least five years. Everyone I knew for most of my growing-up years had married parents. I was in eighth grade before I knew someone whose parents were divorced.
- Loving people. They do nice things for others. Like my mom and dad, who put their family first, who helped family and friends, who volunteered, who gave time and money to numerous charities. I wanted people who were compassionate, caring people.
- College graduates. I loved to learn and wanted my child to have the gift of learning too. I also wanted my child to be able to get a good job someday, to have the best chance in life.

"Okay, this looks like a very good list. I will talk to the attorney I work with and we'll see what we can come up with. There are so many families looking for babies; I'm certain that we'll find a good family for yours."

I left Dr. Hunter's office hoping and praying that we would find the right family. A family that was fun and loving and caring. A family that valued education, truth, and honesty. A family with a strong work ethic and good values. A family that took vacations so the kids could explore the world.

This would be the most important decision of my entire life. But how would I know for sure who was right? How would I know for sure? *Please God, please universe, help me find the right family.*

CHAPTER 23

February 1985

"You know, it's kind of funny that you, who love to talk so much, are teaching a bunch of kids who can't hear you!" I had to tease my sister just a little bit as we drove through the dark early morning to her job at the Utah School for the Deaf, which sat at the foothills of the Wasatch Mountains.

"Oh, I still talk a lot. It's just with my hands," she said, taking it all in stride.

I was glad for the invitation to join Becky at school that day. My days passed by very slowly when I spent most of them in the confines of our one-bedroom apartment. I'd been pretty blue and needed something to lift me up.

Becky's third-grade classroom was spacious—with a capacity of probably thirty students—but she only had five children in her room. As they came in one by one that morning, they were immediately intrigued by my presence, and I was touched by theirs.

"Bauer," they signed with their fast-moving little fingers. "Who is that?" They turned and pointed to me.

I smiled and waved back to them.

"That's Chrisy, my little sister!" Becky signed back to them.

Once everyone was in the room, I joined Becky near her neatly organized desk at the front as she signed to her class: "This is my sister; my little sister, Chrisy. She's going to be helping us out today."

They were delighted to learn that "Bauer" had a sister. One of her students, Maria, looked confused. At only nine years of age, Maria was nearly as wide as she was tall. Her mouth hung open and her large, crooked teeth stuck out. She had a distant, confused look in her eyes much of the time, but she seemed to focus and light up when Becky talked to her or hugged her.

"Your sister?" she signed to Becky with a few moves of her pudgy fingers. "You have a sister?" she asked again and again and pointed to me. Finally, her eyes lit up and she ambled toward me with a big, wide grin on her face. When she reached me, her arms opened wide and she wrapped them around me. My arms reciprocated and we hugged—a good, hearty hug. Then, she tapped my back to let me know that she was done. She smiled wide and went back to her desk. Maria looked so happy; I was happy too.

I touched my growing abdomen as I watched Maria walk back to her desk. *God, please make this baby inside me be healthy. What if the baby has something wrong with it? What if no one wants her then? If something were wrong, I might be too afraid to give my special baby over to someone. But then, how could I take care of a kid with special needs when I don't think I could take care of a healthy one?*

It was hard to put those worries out of my head as I looked at Ryan and wondered about his life and future. Ryan's build was slight and his shoulders hunched. His big brown eyes were his most prominent feature, and they overshadowed his poorly repaired cleft lip. I melted when he looked at me and smiled.

I watched Becky interact with Maria and Ryan and the others; although I didn't know what they are saying, I could tell when she was being serious or stern or funny. I was so impressed as I watched my sister with her kids. Becky was a precious gift to these children— and a precious gift to me.

The busywork Becky gave me—cutting out bulletin board materials, organizing the crayons and marker boxes—made the morning go fast, much faster than it would have if I were sitting alone in the apartment. Lunchtime came quickly, and Becky and I went down the hall to visit the teacher friends who were becoming my friends too.

It was then, in the hallway, that I saw him. I watched in awe as this little boy ambled toward us. He was tiny, about the size of a five-year-old, and walked with the help of crutches. As he got closer,

I could see his large ears protruding from the side of his head. They did so not only because they were big for the size of his head but because of the large hearing aids that were tucked in and behind them, causing them to thrust forward. He had glasses that were big, round, and thick, like soda bottles. He struggled with each step as he walked toward us, but his smile was effortless, beaming.

We met in the middle of the hallway and stopped. "Hi, Andy!" Becky said in sign language and out loud.

Andy smiled even bigger and wider now. He leaned on his crutches with his forearms so his hands were free to sign.

"Hi, Bauer," he signed and said with a strange, nasally voice.

"This is my sister, Chrisy," Becky said.

"Hi, Chrisy." My heart was a big puddle. It was like his little voice and his hands had reached inside me and were pulling on me.

"Nice to meet you!'" I said loudly to Andy. Becky signed this as well.

"Are you here on vacation?" Andy asked.

"Nope, I'm here to go to school," I replied, deciding to leave out the rest of the important details that he wouldn't understand.

He nodded his head and signed that he needed to get going.

"Okay. Bye, Andy," we said as we watched him hobble down the hallway.

"Oh my God, he's so cute and sweet," I said.

"Yeah, isn't he a cutie? He's just amazing. When he was a baby, experts told his parents that he should be institutionalized, that he would never walk or talk or do much of anything. But his parents didn't listen and have been adamant about his education. And look at him now! He's our little celebrity."

"He's amazing. Thank God they didn't listen to the so-called experts, huh."

"Yes, and now his parents are fighting at the legislature to get the state to pay for a teacher that specializes in both the blind and deaf, not just one or the other."

"He's blind too?" I asked.

"Legally blind," Becky said. "He can't see much at all."

Oh, but he sees a lot, I think. He saw goodness in the world and was happy, despite all his obstacles. And he made me see that day that when you are feeling sorry for yourself, the best thing to do is get off your ass and look around at someone less fortunate. He'd made me feel better about myself, my baby, my life. I remembered how incredibly lucky I was.

In just those few minutes, I fell in love with Andy and his parents, who would do anything for their precious boy. And little did I know that Andy and his parents would forever change my life and the life of my baby.

CHAPTER 24

March 1985

The invasion began with little to no warning.

I noticed it as I was lying in the warm, soapy bathtub, my tiny sanctuary in the small apartment that Becky was so graciously sharing with me. I glanced down at my growing belly as it stuck out above the water, a small island in the middle of the ocean. *Was that what I think it was?* I bent my head down and used my left arm to touch it and pull down on the skin for a closer look. Sure as shit, there it was.

There was no denying the deep, red, gash-like line on my right breast. *Damn it.* It was a stretch mark. I had been diligent about putting on lotion and vitamin-E cream each and every night, sometimes day and night. But no matter what armor I put on, it came anyway. And it would be the first of many.

My nice, perky, perfect 32Cs had become large, heavy, melon-like 34DDs. They were big, heavy, and uncomfortable. And now I had the added insult of red lines running over them.

I hated my boobs. I hated the stretch marks. I hated my bulging ass and my stomach, which was like a watermelon ready to burst open. I hated my body, every part of it. On top of it all, my hair looked like shit. I was trying to grow it out, so I hadn't gotten it cut for months. It looked awful, but I figured I might as well have my hair look awful now since the rest of me did.

In the midst of this self-deprecation and loathing, I got a kick in the gut—a real kick in the gut. Soon a sense of awe replaced feelings of self-hatred as I watched my stomach move in ways I never imagined possible. These weren't just kicks; they were gymnastics moves inside my body.

Slowly and forcefully, my baby's legs—or maybe arms—kicked me, like she was stretching out and getting ready to do a flip. I could see her little hand or foot moving under my skin, like a hand under a blanket. After a few of those punches, she really got going. Soon the baby was doing full somersaults and flips inside my womb like an agile little gymnast. My whole abdomen was contorting, moving up and down and sideways. It was like an alien had moved in.

I laughed out loud. "Wow, kid, that's amazing!"

And that seemed to encourage her even more. It was like she was saying to me: *Look, Mom, see what I can do! Ready, Mom? I'm going to do a backflip with a full twist.*

"Becky, get in here," I yelled at the bathroom door. "Hurry!" It was just too good and too amazing to keep to myself.

"Are you okay?" Becky said as she rushed into the bathroom, a look of alarm on her face.

"Yep, I'm okay. I just want you to see this." I pointed to my stomach. "Watch."

As if on command, my child performed her gymnastic routine for Aunt Becky. Rolling, flipping, and twisting—contorting my stomach like I could have never imagined, like a dog moving around under the covers on a bed. We sat—I in the warm water and Becky at the edge of the tub—and watched in wonder as my baby moved underneath my skin and entertained us.

"So do you think it's a boy or a girl?" Becky asked as the movements started to slow down.

"Oh, I don't know. I go back and forth, but I'm having more feelings that it's a boy." I said this aloud, trying to think it. I wanted to convince myself of this because for some reason I felt it would be easier to give up a boy. Even though it was hard to picture myself with a child at all, when I did I could more easily picture myself with a baby girl. I was making myself think that this little gymnast was a boy, but deep down in my core, I was pretty sure it was a girl.

My hands moved onto my belly; I spread my fingers out so I could feel the sensation on the outside as well as the inside. It was miraculous, and I was in awe. I felt bad then for having hated my body and what pregnancy was doing to me. Guilt washed over me in one fell swoop.

Oh, what an ass I am for thinking those selfish things about my body. I was growing another life inside me for another family. That was what mattered.

CHAPTER 25

April 1985

"Hello, little sister!" Becky said cheerfully as soon as she walked into the apartment. "How was your day today?"

"It was okay," I said from my standard position on the right side of the couch, closest to the TV, where I watched countless hours of sitcoms like *Cheers, Who's the Boss?*, and *The Cosby Show*. It was my escape, my best chance each day at eking out a smile or a few laughs. "Same old, same old."

"Well, I've got some potentially good news for you, sis," Becky said as she made the few steps toward me and sat down. "I saw Sally Prouty—Andy's mom—today, and she and her husband, Mike, recently reconnected with some friends of theirs who are looking to adopt a baby."

"Really? What did she tell you about them?" I asked as I pushed myself up and off the couch, intrigued and excited. I hadn't found the right people yet through my doctor, and I was starting to get nervous—very nervous.

"Well, Mike and this guy went to school together—grade school through high school—and they haven't seen each other in a really long time, kind of lost contact. Then this guy—I think his name is Dennis—saw Mike's picture and that article in the paper about Mike lobbying the legislature for a teacher for Andy. How funny is that? So they reconnected and it turns out that this couple has a child they adopted already, but they want to adopt more. They love kids. They tried for many years to have their own and couldn't."

I remembered reading that article about Mike and Andy—cute little Andy from Becky's school who I'd met and fallen in love with. It was on the front page of the *Salt Lake City Tribune*. Mike had addressed the legislature to request funding for a teacher who was certified for both the blind and the deaf.

"Well, if they are friends of the Proutys, they must be good people," I said.

Holy shit. Was this it? Were these friends of Andy's parents meant to be the parents of my child? This seemed like a sign, a very good sign. Dr. Hunter had been presenting potential parents to me for months now and none of them were right. This felt different; this felt right. But how would I know for sure? This would be the most important decision of my life and of my child's life. *God, please help me know if these are the parents for my baby.*

We agreed that Becky would let the Proutys tell their friends that we were interested in learning more about them and meeting them. In the days and weeks ahead, information was exchanged, phone calls made, and a meeting set up.

The waiting was intense. I paced the tiny apartment and the hallway over and over again. Hallway, living room, kitchen, bedroom, repeat. I couldn't sit still.

Although I'd been invited along with Becky to go to the Proutys to meet the Schultzes—the potential parents of my baby—I had decided not to go. I'd agonized over it for days, but in the end I was afraid that I wouldn't say the right things or ask the right things. I was afraid I would just be a mess. But Becky would be perfect.

Becky was my ambassador. I trusted her completely—her instincts, her judgment of character, her communication skills, her ability to keep her emotions in check.

I was only six weeks from my due date and this was the first family we were meeting. I had corresponded with a few couples through Dr. Hunter, but it never went further than that. They didn't feel right to me. None of them had felt right, until now. It was exciting and scary.

What if it didn't work out? How the hell was I going to find the right people? Would I keep the baby because I couldn't find the right family? I'd have to. I'd need to.

As I waited for her return, every headlight I saw flashing through the night and every car door that opened and closed prompted me to run to the window. When Becky finally made it home hours later, her smile and her energy said it all. She had the words to match.

"Oh, Chrisy, they are wonderful! Just wonderful! They are so loving and laid back and nice. They are people who you automatically feel comfortable with. You could just hang out with them. You'd want to be friends with them. They're our kind of people."

I was elated. Becky told me that Dennis and Cindy were both from the Milwaukee area and they met when they were in high school. They both went to college—she for home economics and education degrees. He was finishing his residency to be a family practice doctor. They hoped to someday move back to the Midwest to be near family. I liked that they had Midwestern roots, that they had known each other a long time, and that they wanted another baby so badly. They were close to their families and wanted to be back with them so the baby would have lots of cousins.

Dennis and Cindy had tried for years and years to have a baby and couldn't. They'd adopted their son, Jacob, a year ago, and they loved him so much. They wanted another one to love and raise, to give Jacob a brother or sister.

"Jacob's adoption was also an open adoption, and his birth mom has come to see him a few times. They showed me a photo album that they have with her visiting them. It's just so natural and open. They said that you could do the same—visit, if you want. They will do whatever you want. They'll also make sure that your baby always knows about you."

It was good and comforting to know that I could visit if I wanted. But I didn't know yet if I wanted to do that. It might make it harder than it was already going to be on me and on the baby. How would he or she feel if I just showed up once in a while? *Hey, I'm the other Mom. That might be very confusing to a kid—and too hard for me.*

I hugged Becky and leaned my head on her shoulder. We sat

down on the couch again as I listened to her tell me more about the Schultzes and Proutys, their dinner, and all the wonderful things about the evening.

Dennis and Cindy were members of United Church of Christ, a liberal and accepting church. Cindy was a stay-at-home mom with little Jake and would continue to stay at home with this baby. I liked that she was going to stay home so I wouldn't have to worry about day care on top of everything else. I was all for career, and I hoped desperately to have one someday—but I wanted my baby's mama to be home with her. If I couldn't be with her, her other mom should be as much as possible.

"Dennis and Cindy have an attorney that they used when they got Jacob. I have his name and number. We can meet with him to get the legal stuff started," Becky explained.

As Becky continued to tell me about her evening, we pulled the cushions off the couch and unfurled the hideaway bed from the frame. The mattress was beginning to sway in the middle, where my body lay each night. As soon as it was down, I slipped in between the sheets and laid my head on my pillow.

"Thank you, Becky. I love you so much. I don't know what I would do without you."

What was it about Dennis and Cindy that made me like them right from the moment I heard about them? Was is that they were friends with the Proutys, who were such amazing parents? That they were from the Midwest? That they wanted another baby so badly? That Dennis would be a great provider and that Cindy could stay home with her? That family was so important to them?

Yes, it was those things, but most importantly, it was that thing they called gut instinct. Not only in my gut, though—I felt it in my heart, in my head, in my soul. The Schultzes were it. They were meant to be the parents of my child. It seemed like a miracle that we'd found each other just in time.

CHAPTER 26

April 1985

The big, brown, leather wingback chair made me feel small. That was a nice change, since I felt large and uncomfortable all the time now.

It was my first time in a lawyer's office; it felt awkward and too grown-up for me. Across from me sat Mr. Young, a tall, handsome attorney with a kind and reassuring smile. I glanced at the many framed certificates on the wall behind him as he told me about his experiences with birth moms and adoptive families—it was becoming his specialty. "Dennis and Cindy were great to work with; they're really nice people and great parents," he said.

Knowing that Jacob's mom and other young, pregnant women had sat here in this chair before me offered some solace. I was not the first person to do this. I would not be the last. Since the beginning of time, there had been unexpected pregnancies. I'd read somewhere that almost half of all pregnancies are unplanned. And for a long, long time, there had also been adoptions.

Mr. Young explained the process. "After your baby is born, you will sign a legal document giving up your parental rights. But it's not final. You actually have up to six months to change your mind—during that time you can get your baby back."

I shifted in my chair and placed my hands firmly on my belly, slowly rubbing it in circular motions. He noticed my growing anxiety.

"It doesn't happen very often, but it does happen," he explained. "Moms change their minds."

"That would be really sad for the parents and the baby, wouldn't it?" I said, thinking how traumatic it would be for everyone. I needed to be sure, absolutely sure.

"Yes, it's hard on everyone when that happens, but legal rights favor birth parents."

He explained that he would prepare all necessary documents; within a week of having the baby, I would need to come in and sign.

I would literally be signing a life away—my child's life, part of me. But I did have the option of changing my mind. *Six months. That is a long time. What if I get back to Mitchell or Mankato and then realize I've made a massive mistake? The biggest mistake of my life.* Could I really hop on a plane, show up on Dennis and Cindy's doorstep, and say, "Hi, I changed my mind. I want my baby back!"

That would be devastating to Dennis and Cindy. It would be devastating to my baby. She would not remember that she had lived with me and grown with me for nine months. She would not know how much I loved her. She would not want to go home with me. I would be a stranger to her. Her mother and a stranger all at the same time.

Letter to Dr. Dennis & Mrs. Cindy Schultz—April 29, 1985

Dear Dennis and Cindy,
Hi. I've been meaning to write to you for some time, but it has been hard to do. I have so much that I want to say but can't possibly put it all down on paper. I'll try my best.

Thanks for coming up here to meet with my sister. Through her and Mr. Young, I feel I know you and am secure in my decision to place my baby with you. It has been a difficult and painful decision, but I know that it is best for the baby and for me. I know I could give the baby an abundance of love, but I don't think I could provide all the emotional dedication that he or she deserves. I know you'll provide all of this and more, and it gives me comfort. I also feel good when I think of giving this gift of life to two nice people. I want my child to have the best of everything.

The past eight months have been hard, but I know the hardest is yet to come, when I have to say goodbye. I think what bothers me the most is that my baby won't know how much I love it. I hope you can let her or him know that I love them very much and help him or her realize it was very hard to give up a part of me. I know I'll always be thinking of my child and that we'll be together in my heart.

Becky told me about the photo album of Jacob's with his natural mother in it. I think it's wonderful that you're so open with him. I would like for you to have some pictures of me to give the baby someday. In taking pictures of myself now we are together in a special way. I also have a teddy bear for the baby. I plan to take it in the delivery room with me so it will be there when the baby is born. This will be a special gift that she or he can always treasure. I'm a teddy bear fan and think they can be comforting when you need them.

I sit here and think I'd like to meet you so we could get to know each other, but I'm not ready for that. I don't know how I'll feel after the baby is born either. I hope you can understand this uncertainty. I wonder if I'll want to keep in contact or if it will be easier to just go on with my life. Someday I hope that my child will want to meet me. When he or she is ready, I'll also be ready. I look forward to that day.

I'll always be thinking of you, and you and your children will always be in my prayers. I don't know what more to say other than this—Please give my child a wonderful and happy life. God bless you.

With love,
Christine

Letter from Cindy Schultz—May 8, 1985

Dear Christine,
Thank you so much for your beautiful letter. It is the first thing to go into his or her baby book. Your baby will grow up knowing how much you loved him/her. Having an older brother who is also adopted will make it all that much easier to understand.

We want to especially thank you for giving us your trust. We can easily promise you we will love and cherish your child for the rest of its life. You are a very strong person and we are grateful to you for making our family complete.

We hope and pray that all goes easily for you. You will always be a special person to us.

Love,
Dennis and Cindy

P.S. We would love to hear from Becky as soon as you leave for the hospital if that's okay with you. (Any time of the day or night!)

I read and re-read that short but meaningful letter, and knew that the countdown was on.

I took my checkbook out of my purse and crossed another day off its tiny calendar. Like a prisoner that counts down her days to freedom, I was counting down the days until my body would not be swollen and heavy and bloated and achy and tired—until it would no longer be carrying a baby.

There would be physical relief from the pain and discomfort, but the real emotional pain would have just begun. Would I be able to endure it? Would I be able to let her go to Dennis and Cindy after my body released her?

CHAPTER 27

The second that I saw the envelope I knew it was from him. My hands began to shake. The sadness, anger, and uncertainty I'd felt the last time I talked to Jim all came rushing back. For a few minutes I just held the envelope, wondering if this would make me even more upset. But I had to open it.

Dear Chris,
I'm very sorry about the stupid phone call that I made to you. I think my foolish pride was trying to fight for my baby. My only concern now is your safety and the baby's.
   You were right, we wouldn't give the baby the kind of home it really needs, and I realize that now. My feeling of what we had this summer is still very special to me in my heart. Love to me is the affection and fondness you gave me, which I had never felt before. I know your dream of an education and a career will someday come true because you are a bright and lovable person. Those are some of the things that lead to success.
   I think adoption is the right course to take because if you kept the baby down the line you would resent me and the baby and that wouldn't be fair. School has to be tough right now for you, but just hang in there. No matter what, I am behind you all the way.

   Love,
   Jim

I sat down on the cement sidewalk step next to the mailbox and put my head in my hands. *He is sweet and kind. He is a good person.*

I do love him and I feel remorseful in some ways for choosing this path. Am I being selfish to do this? Can I even do this? If I do decide to keep the baby, Jim will be supportive and we can work it out.

Journal Entry—May 14, 1985

I lie here in the darkness paying minute attention to my body. At every little twinge, I think this could be it. The waiting is really getting to me. I keep saying to myself, "Hurry, hurry, have this baby." I wish it were that easy. Sometimes it still doesn't seem real. I really am going to have a baby. I guess I'm pretty scared.

God, what is it going to be like and feel like? Mentally, I'm trying to prepare for the greatest loss I'm ever going to feel, but when it comes it will be greater than I ever could imagine.

Only nine days to my due date. I hope I don't have to wait that long or longer. What if I'm overdue? I swear I won't be able to handle it. No way. We're supposed to go home in a month and I want time to recover, mostly, mentally. I'm scared to face people—insecurity. I want to be somewhat in control, to know that I won't cry without warning. It's really weird. I get this feeling I'm going to change drastically and I won't be able to communicate with anyone. Oh, please don't let that happen. Don't break down for too long. I've been so strong lately. I'm going to feel so defeated and broken soon.

CHAPTER 28

May 29, 1985
Like a vise being applied to my abdomen and tightened, the first contraction jolted me awake. The room was dark; the alarm clock numbers glowed 5:00 a.m.

Is this it? Was that an official contraction? I'd been having a few Braxton Hicks contractions the past few weeks, but this felt different. This was intense.

I lay still for a while and rubbed my taut belly, feeling for any signs to let me know if this was really it. "Are you ready to come out, sweetheart?" I whispered to her. "I've been waiting for you for so long. But now I don't know if I want you to leave."

Tears streamed slowly down the sides of my cheeks; I held in the deep sobs because I didn't want to make any noise. I didn't want to wake anyone yet. I needed a little more time alone with my baby.

I felt devastated knowing that soon I would be empty. My silent partner who had lived with me, breathed with me, fed off me, listened to me cry, heard my laughter and my anguish, would soon be gone.

I stared through the quiet darkness at the glowing red numbers. Mom and Becky were in the living room on the hide-a-bed—Becky had let me sleep in her room the last week, knowing that sleep had been harder and harder for me to come by.

When half an hour had passed, I started to doubt myself and my body. Maybe that wasn't really a contraction; I'd been sleeping, after all. Maybe it was part of a dream.

Quietly, I waddled to the bathroom and sat down to relieve myself. And then I saw it: the thick bloody mass that looked like snot at the bottom of the toilet. It was the mucus plug that they had told us about in our Lamaze class. This baby was indeed going to come.

I crawled back into bed and spread my hands across my belly. I had stretch marks in so many places but, ironically, not on my belly. As much as I had hated it at times, this big bump was really beautiful; it was a new life, and now it was ready to begin outside of me.

"Hey, little girl," I whispered. "I know I've been telling you over and over again to get out of there, to hurry up. But I'm going to miss you, sweetie. I really am. Please know I love you, okay? I love you so much."

I closed my eyes for just a minute and then another contraction hit. Deep and strong, the wave jolted me again. It had been fifty-five minutes since the last one. Becky would be up in five minutes.

"I'm awake, Beck," I whispered to her as she snuck quietly into the bedroom to get her robe. "It's time. The baby's coming."

Becky flipped on the light and sat gently on the edge of the bed. "You're having contractions?"

"Yes, I've had two."

"Are you sure?"

"I'm pretty sure." For a brief moment I started to doubt myself again because I didn't want to believe it. "And the mucus thingy came out. Remember, they told us that would happen in our Lamaze class? Well, it happened. So two contractions about an hour apart and the mucus thing."

"Yeah, it sounds like this is it. Are you okay?" Becky asked, leaning in to hug me.

"I'm okay. A little scared, but I'm okay."

Though we'd tried to be quiet, we had awakened my mom, who joined us. Worry was written all over her face, but her voice was calm and tender as always. We told her the plan: Becky would go to work for a few hours, then come back. Mom sat down next to me and started rubbing my back.

Before she left for work, Becky reminded me of what we'd learned in Lamaze class to ease the pain and pass the time—a hot shower, walking, eating ice chips, playing games. I showered and got dressed to pass the time. Mom and I got out Scrabble while the *Today Show* hummed in the background. Between placing words, I paced the hallway and stepped in and outside the door.

By ten, I couldn't stand it anymore. I needed to get out of the apartment and to the hospital. I called my sister/birthing coach and asked her to come home. It was time.

The contractions were steady, and I wasn't going to jeopardize my plan to have an epidural; I needed to block at least the physical pain because there was nothing I could do to ease the emotional toll that would be coming. I was and had been feeling pain for nine months, and it would be on a totally different level very soon.

We arrived at the hospital, and everything went like clockwork. We were in plenty of time for the epidural. Becky let me squeeze her hand while the long needle was carefully placed near my spine. I squeezed so hard that I could feel the bones realigning and see her fingers going white. "Good job, honey. You're doing great," she said. She would repeat that many more times, never complaining about the pain I was causing her or the disruption I was.

The epidural worked better than I expected. Soon I felt absolutely nothing from the waist down. *This must be what it's like to be paralyzed.* The only pain left now was mental—intense mental pressure at the knowledge that my baby would be coming out of my body and would be taken away.

"What did Dennis and Cindy say?" I asked Becky as I lay there, numb.

"They said to tell you that they love you and good luck. And they think you are the bravest person in the world."

I wondered what it was like for them, how wonderful it must be to be waiting for the phone call that a baby was coming their way. I'm sure they were also nervous about me changing my mind. I was nervous that I might. I looked at Becky and my mom, sitting on either side of the bed, ready and eager to help me at any second. I'm sure they would be just as eager and ready to help me with this baby, to help me be a mom.

Nurses flowed in and out of my room in a steady stream. They knew the plan and looked at me with sadness and pity. Most of them were surely mothers themselves, and must have wondered how I could do this.

I lost track of how many times I got "checked." I tried not to care anymore how many people had seen my crotch and stuck their fingers up there.

We played cards and watched TV to pass the time. I sucked on lemon drops and ice chips. I closed my eyes and tried to visualize myself pushing.

By quarter to four, I didn't have to visualize any more. They told me finally, "It's time."

The fear that was penetrating my body was also visible in the eyes of my mother. She was scared for me. She knew what childbirth was like; she'd been through it four times. She leaned over, gave me a hug, and told me she loved me. "It's going to go just fine. You're going to be okay."

"I don't know what I'd do without you, Mom."

She left the room as I had requested. I didn't tell her the real reason I didn't want her in there. The real reason was that I didn't want her to see me in pain. I didn't want her to have to watch all this and then see me give her grandchild away—her first grandchild.

The nurses began to bustle about the room. A cart with warm towels and instruments was brought in alongside a bassinet. The bed was repositioned to give me back support, so I could lean forward and push.

Soon, I was spread-eagled, a group of nurses and Dr. Hunter at the bottom of the bed, Becky at my side. I still felt nothing at all, so they had to tell me when to push.

"Come on, Christine, push," they said. "Push."

Becky too cheered me on. "You can do it, Chrisy."

I pushed. I pushed and pushed. I held Becky's hand and I cried. I worked and worked at getting this baby out of me. Though I couldn't feel the pain, I could feel pressure, lots of pressure.

"We see a bit of black hair, here. It's starting to crown, Christine.

You're getting there. Now, we really need to you to work and push as hard as you can."

I shouted, gritted my teeth, and bore down until I felt like every blood vessel in my face was going to burst and my eyes were going to bulge out of their sockets. I did this again and again, each time depleting my energy reserve.

And then I felt a great release.

"The head's out, the head's out. Good job, Christine." The crew was like a little cheering section at the bottom of the bed. "Great job. Now we need you to push again, okay? You're almost there."

I flopped back into the bed, knowing that it was almost over. This moment that I had been counting down to for nine months was almost here.

"I can't. I can't do it. I can't do it anymore," I said, feeling completely despondent.

"Come on, Chrisy," Becky encouraged. "You can do it. You can do this. It's almost over. You've done all this work. You can't stop now."

She was right. I couldn't stop with this baby sticking halfway out of me. But I knew after those last few pushes, that would be it. My baby would no longer be inside me. She would no longer be connected to me. She would not need me to eat and to breathe. She would survive without me. She would be taken from me. *She will be gone and I will be alone.*

God, help me do this. Please, God, help me, I prayed silently as lifted my shoulders, leaned forward, and pushed with all my might. With this last push, I felt a tremendous release of pressure and I heard a beautiful cry.

And then I heard the doctor say those three words:

"It's a girl."

He repeated, "A perfect little girl," as he quickly looked her over.

Instinctively and without hesitation in that split second, I reached down between my legs and touched her. I was in awe at the miracle of it all—this beautiful little life that I had created; this beautiful baby girl that I had made.

I watched as they quickly wiped her off and swaddled her in a warm blanket. It seemed a little rough on this fragile little being. Instinctively, I held out my arms.

The nurse hesitated and looked over to Dr. Hunter. It wasn't part of the plan. I had not planned to hold her.

Dr. Hunter nodded to the nurse, and she placed the baby in my folded arms. She was so warm and tiny and beautiful.

I had not planned to hold her, but it was the most natural thing in the world. How could I not touch the child who had been living and growing with me, who had been kicking and turning inside me for nine months?

I gazed at her in amazement, suddenly overwhelmed by a sea of exhaustion and a flood of emotions. I teetered between tremendous relief for delivering a healthy baby and deep despair and anguish that I would be letting her go.

Becky leaned against me. Together we stared in awe at this new, tiny little life lying in my arms.

"Hello, Elizabeth. Welcome to the world," I whispered. Elizabeth was my confirmation name, and it was my way of giving her a bit of me.

"Chrisy, she's so gorgeous. You did such a great job, sweetie. So great."

"Yes. She's beautiful. She's a miracle, isn't she?"

With my finger, I gently touched her nose and her cheeks. I kissed her on her tiny nose and head and turned her so Becky could do the same.

And then I held out my arms and nodded to the nurse to take her.

"Goodbye, sweet baby girl."

CHAPTER 29

Much to Becky's dismay, she and I shared our little-girl daisy-themed bedroom growing up. She was six years older, so I was admittedly an annoyance to her for the most part. But on many nights, after the lights were out and the house was quiet, we would put aside our difference in years and our sibling rivalries and play.

With our beds just feet apart, we would grab our pint-sized stuffed animals and create little fantasy worlds and characters, staging small weddings, wars, parties, and plays with our make-believe people. We'd play and giggle and pretend until we'd inevitably hear the loud, deep voice from across the hall shout: "Get to bed!"

How on earth could he hear us? we'd wonder. My dad had gone to bed hours ago—it was like he had radar ears. He was always onto us.

Our laughter would quickly die down and we'd reluctantly climb back into our separate beds. After a few minutes of quiet, Becky would turn and whisper ever so faintly to me: "Do you want to give backrubs?"

"Sure," I'd whisper back, thinking of the gentle, soothing backrub my mom had given us earlier.

"You rub my back first," Becky would say, turning onto her stomach and hiking up her pajama top.

"How long?" I asked as I climbed back over to her bed and started rubbing her back. I'd watch the minutes pass by on the alarm clock that sat on the nightstand between our beds. One minute. Two minutes. Three minutes. Finally, after ten, I'd stop and whisper, "Okay. It's my turn."

"Hey, it's my turn," I'd say again, nudging her.

Nothing. She wouldn't budge. She was sleeping. So I'd climb back into my bed, disappointed and dejected, and watch my sister sleep, or pretend to, loving her and hating her at the same time. *She owes me so many back rubs.*

Many years later, she more than made up for them.

CHAPTER 30

May 30, 1985
The room was eerily quiet and still. My mom and Becky were in the lounge down the hall trying to sleep, and except for the occasional sounds of the nurses at their station, it was quiet. I was alone, truly alone, for the first time in nine months, and the isolation was gripping. My partner, my womb-mate, was gone, and my longing for her was deep and painful. My hands clung to the jiggly, loose flesh where she used to be. That was all that was left now, an empty parcel to remind me what had been inside.

I missed her. I ached for her. It was an ache that pounded in my heart, my womb, my soul, my head. A part of me was gone, like a phantom limb. It was there but not there. I pictured her in a bassinet all by herself just down the hallway and had to keep telling myself: "Don't go down there. Don't go down there."

It would have been so easy to get up and walk that way, but if I did, I was afraid there would be no turning back.

My mom and Becky had spent time down in the nursery holding her, and they said she was being well cared for by the nurses. But it didn't seem like enough. She needed her mom. She needed bonding. I'd heard and read about bonding and the need for it to take place right away—those first hours, days, and months were critical. But if I made that bond, there would be no turning back. The more I held her, the more I couldn't want to let her go.

I could still change my mind; it was my right to change my mind. The lawyer even said so. I had six months.

The door opened and broke up my thoughts. A new face, another nurse in white uniform. "Hello, Christine." She walked up next to the bed and apologized for having to do what she was about to. I looked away as she pulled back the covers, placed her fingertips on my abdomen, and pushed down in circular motions, again and again, to make the uterus contract and expel what was left inside. It hurt, just like my swollen crotch and bottom hurt and my breasts hurt. But these external injuries were nothing compared to the hurt I was feeling inside.

"Have you slept at all?" she asked.

"No, not really," I admitted.

"Let me get you something else to help you sleep," she said, and after a brief pause added: "Your baby is doing just fine. I went and checked on her a little bit ago, and she's doing just fine. She's a beautiful baby, and you should feel proud of what you've done."

Her words provided a brief bit of comfort, like a thin blanket tossed on a freezing body. Not enough to save me, but enough to slightly ease the pain.

I wanted Elizabeth's parents to come and get her. She needed to be with them; I needed for her to be with them, before it was too late. Before I changed my mind. As soon as Becky and my mom appeared in my room in the morning, I asked Becky to call the Schultzes.

The plan had been for them to come two days after Elizabeth was born. But I couldn't let her sit down there in the nursery by herself. I couldn't stand it. Becky called, and just over twenty-four hours after she was born, Dennis and Cindy came to the hospital to meet their new daughter and take her home. Becky let me know when they'd arrived.

"Okay, but I want to see her—I need to see her—one more time, Becky."

I needed to talk to her, to tell her again how I felt. Becky went to the nursery and came back into my room a few minutes later, cradling the tiny bundle of pink blanket ever so gently in her arms. She brought my baby to me, and I took her and tenderly held her warm, tiny body in my arms, nestling her against my chest.

She was so incredibly perfect; a flawless specimen of life. Life that was pure and innocent and vulnerable and fragile. A life that I was entrusting to someone else.

I reached up, gently touched her nose, and outlined her heart-shaped lips. I brushed her tiny, perfect ears and caressed her silky little head. I drank in her sweet baby-powder smell. And through my tears, in my softest, gentlest voice, I whispered to my daughter:

"I love you so much, baby girl. I love you. I love you more than words can say and more than you'll ever understand. You're such a beautiful, perfect baby, and I want you to have a beautiful life. Your new mom and dad will love you just as much as I do, okay? And they'll give you a great home and a great life. I can't give you a great life right now. I hope you'll understand that this is best for both of us, okay? And I know we'll be together again someday. I promise."

She opened her eyes then and looked into mine, like she was telling me it was okay.

Then I kissed her goodbye. I was crying so hard that I could barely find and push the nurse's button. But it was time to let her go; otherwise I would want to hang on forever.

Becky came to my bedside and we both snuggled the little lady in my arms one more time. "You're doing the right thing," my sister assured me. She kissed me on the cheek as I slowly and carefully extended my arms and handed over Elizabeth. Becky took her from my arms; tears streaming down her face, she walked my seven-pound bundle of life and love down the hallway into the arms of her new mom and dad.

Journal Entry—May 30, 1985

Yesterday, I gave birth to the most beautiful baby girl. Her birth was such a miracle that all nine months and everything I have gone through were worth it. Right when she was born, I knew I'd done the right thing by having her. I reached down and touched her and then they laid her on my tummy and I got to hold her.

Oh, God, she's perfect, so precious. I only held her for a minute and then they took her to be cleaned up. Next, I cried, tears of both joy and sadness—joy because I gave life and she's so healthy, sadness because I lost a part of myself. I feel very proud, though. I brought a life into the world. I want to hold the memory of her birth like a photograph. It was so special. She's so beautiful, just beautiful. She was born at 4:39 p.m., weighing 7 lbs and 19 inches long.

Becky was a huge help. I could not have made it without her. We cried together when the nurse took the baby. Mom, I'm so thankful she's here. I need the most important people that I love near me. Mom and Becky both held the baby today. They talked to her and let her feel their love.

Then, I held her again today. I hadn't planned to hold her at all, but when I saw her, there was no way that I couldn't. Before her mom and dad came to get her, I knew that I had to talk to her and let her know how much I love her. I wish I could capture my feelings better on this paper but there are really no words to describe how I felt. Holding her was so right—it felt so good. Oh, how I love her. And I feel so empty and deserted now. I have to go now because my thoughts are being replaced and drowned out by tears.

CHAPTER 31

June 6, 1985

My eyes followed the baby in the stroller as was she wheeled right in front of me. I stopped in my tracks. Pangs of guilt and longing washed over me as I stared at the infant, covered with a pink blanket and wearing a pink-and-white, flowered skullcap. Her tiny face poked out of the stroller like a spring tulip pushing through the earth.

She was a newborn, just like my little Elizabeth. Elizabeth, who was a week old now. I wondered if Dennis and Cindy had taken her out like this yet, if they had started showing her to the world. I thought how proud I would be to be able to show my baby to the world. Everyone loves babies. I hoped Dennis and Cindy were showing her off like crazy and that her older brother liked her.

Becky and Mom stopped, too, their eyes moving to the baby. "Come on, let's try the Limited store," Becky said in an attempt to distract me. I didn't say anything. I just followed her as she headed in the direction of the store, brushing aside my desire to follow the lady and her baby.

The mall was crowded on this weekday afternoon. Mothers with young children and groups of teenagers scooted up and down escalators and in and out of stores. Music played over the speakers; sounds of chatter and laughter filled the air. I was trying hard to enjoy it, trying hard to enjoy not being pregnant anymore, trying hard to be a nineteen-year-old college student simply looking for some much-needed clothes.

It had been a long time since I'd bought anything except ugly maternity bras and underwear, and I think Becky and Mom were on a mission to get me back out into the world. I smiled for the first time in a week as they handed me things to try on, getting into the spirit as best I could. This reminded me of old times, of our shopping trips when I was a little girl. Every spring and every fall, Mom, Becky, and I would drive an hour east on Interstate I-90 to Sioux Falls—the retail mecca of our humble state of South Dakota—spend the day shopping, and have lunch. We always had fun, but I'd hated trying on the clothes.

"Remember when we used to go to Sioux Falls shopping?" I shouted to them through the dressing room curtain.

"You were the worst at trying stuff on," Becky said, laughing.

"I know I was. And I still am. I hate it."

I *really* hated it today, when the small dressing room space put me so close to a mirror where I had to see my body with its red stretch marks, that jiggly, loose skin where my baby, my precious little baby, used to be. My baby's name was no longer Elizabeth; Becky learned from Cindy that they had named her Kathryn Anne. I liked that too; but I did feel a bit sad that they had changed her name, mostly because it was something I had given her.

My shopping partners were enjoying their role of wardrobe consultants. They kept handing me a steady stream of clothes—shirts, shorts, and jeans—over and under the dressing room door. As I tried the clothes on, they gave their opinion on fit, style, and size. My regular size was, of course, too tight and barely zippable, but the next size up fit pretty well. But we all knew that my size would change soon; I was carrying extra weight from that beautiful little baby. The weight would fade away soon enough.

After too many minutes of trying on clothes, we decided on a few key pieces that would get me through the next few months—from an outside standpoint, anyway. What I needed was something to get me through on the inside, where I was exposed and hurting.

We left the store carrying packages in our hands. I also carried guilt. How could I enjoy buying new clothes for myself and worrying about trivial things when I had just turned a vulnerable little life over to people I really didn't even know? I felt selfish and doubtful.

Oh God, did I do the right thing? I kept coming back to that question as we left the retail world and headed back to the apartment, my cocoon.

CHAPTER 32

The sun was bright and the sky as brilliant blue as could be the day we drove out of Ogden, Utah, a mere eleven days after Katie was born. My mom had flown home a few days earlier, so it was Becky and me making the road trip home to Mitchell. It was a thousand-mile journey that would take us through the corner of Utah and across Wyoming and South Dakota.

As Becky eased the car through the streets and away from the city, the tears began to ease their way out of my eyes and down my cheeks. It was hard to leave—so much had happened here. I grew up so much here. I gave birth here. I was leaving my week-and-a-half-old baby here. I was leaving not only a huge emotional chunk of myself but an amazing physical part of myself as well.

It hurt to go, but I knew I had to. I was going back to my life and my dreams, and my baby's new parents had started theirs. I envisioned Cindy and Dennis holding her, feeding her, changing her diapers. I pictured them dressing her in cute outfits and taking her for walks in her stroller at the foothills of these mountains, surrounded by the colorful wildflowers that were in bloom.

If I stayed in Ogden, these thoughts would consume me. The urge to see Katie would be too great. Putting this distance between us would make it less tempting to change my mind—even though I had signed the paperwork giving parental rights to Cindy and Dennis, I still could. I had six months.

Becky sensed my emotions and silently reached over and held my hand, just as she had done at the airport on the day we left South Dakota to come here. No words were needed; we let the music from the radio fill the space surrounding us. Sting's song "If You Love Somebody Set Them Free" came on. *Free, free, set them free.*

I gazed at the mountains and thought about how much I would miss them, how happy I was that my daughter would get to grow up surrounded by them. I hoped she would find solace in them as I did, as well as adventure and fun. I could have used more time here in the mountains to heal my wounds, but Becky was ready to go home and I had to honor that. She had let me encroach on her life for five months, so it was her time now.

We passed the time on our drive by playing games, like identifying different states' license plates and making up rhymes. Other times we simply soaked in the scenery. Rather than taking the more direct way home, we'd chosen a more scenic route that took us north out of Utah and into the Jackson Hole, Wyoming, area of Grand Teton National Park. We made it there in about four and a half hours and spent the rest of the day enjoying the spectacular mountains, pristine lakes, and pine trees.

Bright and early the next morning, we began our thirteen-hour journey to Mitchell. With each hour that passed and each mile that we got closer to home, I got more and more nervous. I'd be seeing my dad and brothers for the first time since Christmas; we'd never really talked in depth about my decision. Would we talk about it now? Or would we try to act like nothing had happened? I hoped we could talk about it at least a little bit. I'd also be seeing Jim; I'd need to talk to him about the baby and how he was feeling. I wondered how I'd feel about him now.

When we pulled up in front of 1007 Mitchell Boulevard, Mom, Dad, Brad, Curt, DaNette, and the dogs all came out to greet us. My mom had a rose for each of us girls. When we got inside, there were a few homemade signs that said "Welcome Home" and "Yay, You Are Back!"

There is truly no place like home, and it felt so good to be there. We ordered pizza and had beer and then went to the lake to check out Brad's new house. We did and talked about a lot of things, but we didn't talk at all about the family member who wasn't with us.

Journal Entry—June 13, 1985

It seems strange to be sitting in this room, in this house, in this town. But it feels good. I can't believe I'm home. It doesn't seem like it was six months ago that I left here. I do feel different, but I am different. I went through a lot. I'm doing pretty good though, a lot better than I anticipated. I'm proud of what I've done, for I know it was right for Kathryn (they changed her name). She is two weeks old today. I wonder what she looks like now. I still hold the memory of her in my arms very near to my heart and think of it every day. I haven't cried since I've been home and I almost feel guilty because I haven't. Is that right? I don't know. I guess I'm stronger than I think.

CHAPTER 33

June 1985

The warm breeze of the June evening washed over us as we sat side by side on the steps at the public beach, looking out onto Lake Mitchell. The lake was a small, man-made reservoir that served as a key recreation point for the residents of our small town and a key party destination for local teens throughout the years. There was no party today that I could see. Just the hum of jet skis and fishing boats that filled the air, as did the occasional buzz of mosquitoes. From our vantage point, we had a good view of the west end of the lake, where the sky was just beginning to paint itself in sunset hues of oranges and blues.

I was glad for the peacefulness of our surroundings; it made me a bit less nervous as I sat next to Jim. It was the first time we had seen each other since the winter holidays, and so much had happened since then. He wanted to hear again about Kathryn and the delivery, so I told him the story, trying hard to convey all the adequate details and feelings.

"She's so beautiful. Just this perfect little baby. And her parents are really wonderful."

He put his arm around me and gave me a quick squeeze around the shoulders. "It sounds like we did the right thing; I hope and pray we did the right thing," he said. "Again, I'm sorry for doubting you and calling you about changing your mind and raising her, but there is part of me that wanted to keep her, to be a dad."

Same with me. I did too! I thought to myself.

"I know. I get it. I so get it. I wanted to be her mom and watch her grow up too, but I need to finish growing up myself."

We sat in silence for a while before shifting to small talk about mutual friends and what was going on around town. Jim squinted, pursing his lips to hold the cigarette in his mouth in place as he pulled another out of the pack. He lit that one off the one in his mouth and I noticed the yellow stains between his fingers, evidence of his chain-smoking. I looked at it as I lit my own cigarette and felt like a jerk for judging. But at least I wasn't lighting it off of another one, I justified, at the same time flogging myself for starting again. Why did I do it? I knew the answer, though. In some odd way, it helped ease my pain. I wasn't alone in that; I'd heard some troubling news through the grapevine.

"Now, don't get mad if I ask you this, but I heard that you've been drinking again?"

"This has been pretty stressful, you know."

"I just worry about what could happen."

"Don't worry about it. I'll be fine."

I hoped he would be fine. And even though I was just looking forward to moving on and getting away from here, I cared for Jim very much. We had created a life—a monumental thing to share with someone. It was the beginning and the end.

We didn't see each other much after that night. I stuck to hanging out with and enjoying my family and a few close friends, especially Diane, whom I'd known since kindergarten.

Nearly every day that summer, I'd walk to her house, just a few blocks down the quiet, tree-lined streets of Mitchell Boulevard. I'd pass the other ranch-style houses and the park where we had played for entire days during our grade school years. Diane's family put in a pool when we were in high school; that summer, just as we had in high school, we spent hours there, soaking up the sun, eating freeze pops, watching soap operas on the TV we brought outside, and discussing life. It was a safe and comforting routine as I adjusted to being a nineteen-year-old again, rather than being an expectant mother.

We also went out at night sometimes; Diane would talk me into hitting the bars and going to a few parties. I'd have fun for a little while, and then it would hit me head-on—a freight train full of guilt. This incredible culpability would roll over me and I would feel bad for feeling good. Having fun seemed so wrong when I was still grieving my loss. No one understood my love for my baby. No one understood this grief that stood right beside relief.

    I never lived at home again after that summer. Although I was closer to my family now more than ever, I never went back to Mitchell for more than school breaks. I loved college, my friends, my job, my life. I had no reason to go back. I just kept moving forward.

CHAPTER 34

Spring 1986

The clicking of keyboards (we had Macintosh computers!), ringing telephones, and excited young voices—the sounds in the *MSU Reporter* newsroom—were like rock and roll to my ears. It was music that made me feel happy, energized, alive.

Our campus newspaper became my place of employment and my hangout at Mankato State University when I went back to school my sophomore year. It didn't take me long to feel that it was home, that I belonged there. It felt so good to have a purpose and a passion. Not only was I having fun as a reporter, but I was getting *paid*—twenty-five dollars for each article that I wrote for the newspaper. I was blown away by the fact that I was getting paid to write, paid to do what I loved.

Seeing my byline, "By Chris Bauer, staff writer," next to the stories that I wrote was incredibly gratifying. Just a few months earlier, I had declared Mass Communications as my major and Political Science as my minor. I'd always loved writing and had written for my high school newspaper, *Kernel News*. I got good grades in English, was a news junkie, and wanted to save the world. My interest, education, and career stars had aligned and were pointing me in the right direction.

The *Reporter* published twice a week, on Tuesdays and Thursdays, and had a circulation of eight thousand. We were an important part of campus life, especially on Thursdays, when the classified ads announced parties for the weekend. Under the headline *Parties*, you could find valuable information. "Party! 25 kegs. $5 cover. 225 Bradley Street." "$5 all you can drink. Best party! 550 State Street." We served a purpose. Besides delivering the campus news, we provided the social networking of our time.

Before, between, and after my classes, I was at the *Reporter* office. I went there not only to work on my stories, but to talk politics, parties, news, and newspapers with the other staffers. I loved all of it, especially meeting new people and learning and writing about interesting topics and issues.

I met and wrote about people like Jim Chalgren, a gay man who founded MSU's Alternative Lifestyles office, only the second such center at a U.S. university when it opened in 1977. He was the first openly gay person I had met, and I admired his bravery and tireless efforts to challenge prejudice, educate students, and change policies. Another favorite interview was Dr. Margaret Preska, MSU's president. She was the highest-ranking professional woman I had ever met, and I respected her so much. Dr. Preska was not only poised and astute, but she was also warm and friendly and made me feel smart and important when I interviewed her.

I was learning and telling so many people's stories, yet I told very few people my own. Only a few people knew about Katie and my journey over the past few years. She was such a huge part of me, part of what I carried with me always, yet I didn't talk about her. I didn't know how.

On college campuses, children—little, big, or in between—are pretty much out of sight and therefore out of mind, so it wasn't hard for me to tuck my baby away deep in my heart. I kept my head down and focused on my work and studies and life as a college student. I acted as if that was all I was—but I was so much more than that. I was a mother, but I just couldn't talk about it.

May 29, 1986

Dear Cindy, Dennis, and Katie,
I hope you are all fine. I've been thinking of you all day today. I had meant to send the birthday card and letter earlier so that it would have arrived today, but I just felt I had to wait until today to be able to write.
It's hard to believe that Katie is already one year old. This year has

gone by so fast; in some ways it seems like Katie was born just yesterday and in others it feels like long ago.

Today was a hard day, but it was happy along with sad. It is comforting to know in my heart that she is loved and protected, and I know in my heart that you are wonderful parents. I'm sure there was a fine celebration for this special occasion; although I was not there in person, my heart was with you all day.

I talked to Becky tonight and she said that you had called. Thank you for including me in your day. It helps to know you are thinking of me at the same time I am thinking of you.

I often wonder what Katie looks like, as I'm sure she is changing and growing so fast. I also wonder what her personality is like, what she does, and the list goes on and on.

My mom told me today that she had visited you and showed me Katie's picture. She is beautiful! And I can tell that she is happy. It is amazing how much she has grown and changed. I have to admit, I think she looks like me.

I was out in Ogden for spring break and thought of coming to see you. But I decided it was not the right time. I'm sure someday we will meet, and I look forward to that day.

I had a nice time out in Utah. It was so good to be with Becky and also to see old friends. The mountains were amazing. I'd forgotten how pretty it is out there.

Life in Minnesota is pretty good. I really like school and have finally decided on a major in Mass Communications. When I started school in the fall I was a little apprehensive about everything but it has turned out great. I've adjusted well and truly feel my future is going in the direction that I want it to take.

I know I made the right decision and I'm happy that you're happy. I guess I should be going now. For being a Mass Communications major I sure don't feel that I can write very well. I have lots of others things to say but it's hard to put on paper. But the most important thing to say is: "I love you."

Please give Katie a hug and a kiss for me (many of them).

God Bless, Love Chrisy

CHAPTER 35

October 12, 1987
Wearing a surgical cap and gown, my brother Curt stood at the thick glass window of the hospital nursery and held up his new baby girl for all of us to see. It was just like they did in the movies—proud parent showing off the new baby from behind the glass. Curt was finally able to show us his newborn daughter, who they'd named Cami, after many long hours of waiting and a long and painful labor for DaNette.

At the urging of my parents, I'd come home for the weekend to meet my new niece or nephew and to celebrate my birthday. The baby was due several weeks earlier, so we thought for sure it would arrive by the start of the weekend. Now it was Sunday evening and I needed to get on the road soon for my four-hour drive back to school.

I met my dad and mom at the hospital along with members of my sister-in-law's side of the family. There was excitement in the air; everyone had been eager for this grandchild to arrive. I was happy and excited too, even though it was strange and difficult in so many ways. This was the second grandchild on DaNette's side of the family, technically the second on the Bauer side too. But no one mentioned that. On the Bauer side, Cami would be thought of and talked about as the first grandchild. I understood it, but it made me sad because it made me long for Katie.

I felt the buzz and excitement as the families talked about this new addition to the world and thought of how different it was from my experience just a year and a half ago. It wasn't just a layer of glass between me and Curt; it was a world of difference between us.

Curt's smile revealed both pride and relief as he held Cami carefully in his arms and then came closer for us to see. Everyone gathered around and made oohs and ahhs, and for good reason. She was beautiful. He held his healthy baby girl swaddled tightly in a pink blanket, and it reminded me, of course, of the second time—and last time—I saw Katie, when I held her in my arms and told her goodbye. She was wrapped up like that too, all snuggled, warm, and protected. But I didn't get to show her off to anybody.

As I looked at Curt's little girl, I thought of how she and Katie could have been friends and playmates. My little girl and Cami could have been best buddies. They could have played together, hung out with grandma, and had sleepovers. Maybe they could still be friends someday, or at least get to know each other. I hoped so.

I fought back the longing and the sadness I felt and willed my mind to think positive thoughts. Katie had her own cousins and another sibling now, and I had a beautiful little niece who shared my birthday. It was a great twenty-first-birthday present.

I smiled and waved to my brother and then hugged my mom and dad goodbye. It was time for me to head back to school. It was where I was meant to be, but it wasn't easy. Loss never is, and it never goes away.

CHAPTER 36

December 1988

My mom always went above and beyond for me and for all of us kids. Like when she chartered an airplane from Mitchell to Mankato in order to make it to my college graduation ceremony and celebration.

"What? You're coming?" I screamed into the phone.

It was a great surprise after a long and stressful few weeks. Not just my *final* final exam stress, but real life-and-death stress. Initially my mom wasn't going to come to my graduation—no one from my family was going to come—because my dad had suffered a heart attack and had just been released from the hospital.

"Your dad and I talked about it and realized that I just couldn't miss it," she explained. "We missed Becky's college graduation because we were traveling and we don't want to miss this. So I'm chartering a plane for the day. I can fly in for the ceremony, come to your party for a little bit, and then fly back home at the end of the day."

As excited as I was about her coming, I was equally sad that my dad wouldn't be there. My dad's first heart attack had been thought to be mild at first, but it turned into several emergencies, a near-death experience, and nearly a month in the hospital. We rallied around him, and I'm sure it was his stubbornness that brought him through it.

As I sat in the gym listening to the speeches from Dr. Preska and others, I thought about how fast the past four and a half years had gone and how incredibly good they had been. These college years had been, hands down, the best of my life. It was here that I really found myself.

I'd spent countless hours in the *Reporter* office and written hundreds of news stories for the paper. Later, as news editor, I'd spent hundreds of hours assigning stories, working with reporters, editing pieces, and laying out the paper for the printer along with the team. Many nights, we were at the newspaper office until one or two in the morning, putting together the newspaper and bonding as friends and colleagues.

Yet even with my long hours at the newspaper office, I'd rarely ever missed a class in four years. I truly loved school; I loved learning and studying and was proud to graduate with a 3.4 GPA. I received cum laude honors.

I hoped that someday I'd be able to tell my daughter all of this, that she would be proud of me. That maybe it would help her understand that I just couldn't be a mom at the same time. I wasn't mother material during these years.

I was not, however, all work and no play. I also managed to squeeze in plenty of parties and countless nights of drinking beer, smoking cigarettes, and solving the world's problems with friends. I loved so many of these people and I felt so loved and respected in return.

With my diploma in my hand on my way back to my seat, I spotted my mom. She was beaming with pride at this daughter who had caused her so much pain over the years. I was so happy to be bringing her joy today.

"This is our diploma," I said to her as we embraced after the ceremony.

"You never know; I could still get one," she said, only half joking. She had quit college just a few credits shy of graduating to marry my dad. Like so many women of her generation, the only degree she got from her university was an MRS degree. Her dreams were shelved so that my dad could pursue his. She took a few classes here and there over the years, but raising four children and running a busy household didn't leave much time for classes and homework. That's why the diploma I clutched in my hands was so important and not only mine—it was for my mom, and for Katie too. I could not have achieved this degree, at least in this way—on this campus, with these friends, finding my passion—if I had been raising her. I hoped that someday Katie would understand, that she would pursue her dreams and goals and find her own passion.

CHAPTER 37

May 1989

I checked and rechecked the schedule that I held tightly in my hands. I had also called Metro Transit the day before just to make sure I was reading the schedule correctly. Yes, they said, I had it right: 7:25 a.m. at Seventy-Sixth and Lyndale.

The bus would be there any minute. I didn't ride the school bus as a kid. We walked or my mom drove us. And Mitchell didn't have public transportation. So it was a big day for me—a Metro Transit bus ride to my first day of work in downtown Minneapolis.

It was not just *work* or *a job*, though; it was the start of my career. I was so excited I could hardly stand it. I couldn't eat breakfast and could barely choke down my beloved coffee. This was it—what I had been working toward for so long. I waited on the bench at the bus stop on the busy street right outside my apartment building. Dressed in my crisp blue suit, with its slightly-above-the-knee skirt and tailored jacket complete with shoulder pads, I felt good. I felt empowered. I felt confident.

My mom would love it all. I wish she could see me. She was nearly as excited as I was about my job in the big city. She bought me the suit when she came up the previous week and helped me move into my one-bedroom apartment in the suburb of Richfield.

My nylon-clad legs glided across each other as I crossed and recrossed them. My sweaty hands clutched my brown leather briefcase—a graduation gift from Becky. Finally, I saw the bus round the corner and stood to greet it. It was exactly 7:25.

Gingerly I climbed the steps, put the bus fare into the box, and took an empty seat toward the front. I wanted easy access to the driver if needed. I looked around at my fellow passengers, mostly men and women in suits. Many were shrouded by their morning newspapers. Others were immersed in books or magazines. Some were plugged into their Sony Walkmans.

I was free from any reading materials, plugged into only the vibrant city that flashed by me. Looking out the front and side windows, I took in the tree-lined scenery as the bus wound its way through the streets of Richfield and south Minneapolis and made its way into downtown.

Along the way, we passed by several buildings and churches that housed day care centers and preschools. I watched moms and dads carrying babies in car seats or holding hands with their toddlers as they made their way inside. Katie then entered my mind. I was glad that Cindy had stayed home with Katie and her siblings over the years; it was one less thing for me to worry about. I knew Katie was being cared for and loved as I finished school, and now as I started my job. I wouldn't be here on this bus, heading to this job, if I had kept her. Was that selfish? Had I been selfish all these years? *No. No, I can't think that way. I know Cindy and Dennis do not think I was selfish. I gave them the best gift ever.*

I turned my focus back to the present. I didn't want to miss my stop. The closer we got to tall buildings, the closer I got to the edge of my seat. When the bus finally stopped at Marquette and Eighth Street, I popped out of my seat and took the big steps off the bus. My smile was surely as big as my stride as I walked north up Eighth Street to Dayton's Department Store, a landmark and cultural center point in the city.

I paused for a moment next to the IDS Center, Minneapolis's tallest building. Standing on the sidewalk, I leaned my head back and looked up at this massive steel-and-glass structure, remembering my elevator ride and visit to the fiftieth floor as a child on family vacation years ago. I closed my eyes for a second and remembered watching in awe as the lights of the city spread out for miles before me. I remembered thinking how cool it would be to live in a city with so many lights, with so many restaurants and shops and theaters.

Now, here I was, walking by this building on my first day of work, just like Mary Tyler Moore. I thought of Mary as an old friend who had ventured into Minneapolis and forged a career. I met her sitting in our family room, watching her on TV every week, when I was ten years old. I remembered her and Rhoda fondly. How cool I thought these women were—these women who had these great jobs, great apartments, and great fun in Minneapolis.

I couldn't stop the words and the music from coming into my head as I crossed Nicollet Mall to Dayton's Department Store: *Who can turn the world on with her smile? Who can take a nothing day, and suddenly make it all seem worthwhile? Well it's you, girl, and you should know it. With each glance and every little movement, you show it!*

If only I had a hat, I would have thrown it up in the air, just like Mary did in the same spot. Instead, I just wore my big smile as I walked into the Dayton's employee entrance, where I received my ID badge and was directed into the store toward the elevators.

I paused to drink it all in and admire the splendor of my new employer's lobby. Grand crystal chandeliers hung from the ceiling every ten feet and marble tiles graced the floor. An immense floral arrangement sat on a round table in the center aisle, flanked by perfume and cosmetic counters on either side. What an incredible way to start the workday.

Realizing I might be looking like a geek just gazing down an empty aisle as employees streamed by me, I got myself together and walked with them toward the elevator. Someone punched the button and a few people got off with me on the eighth floor. A sign pointed left for Human Resources and right for the auditorium.

Again, my memories made me smile. The store's auditorium was where the magic happened, where Dayton's transformed its auditorium into a fantasy wonderland every year. Around the same time I was watching Mary Tyler Moore, my mom, Becky, and I had come to Minneapolis to shop and visit Dayton's eighth-floor auditorium, transformed into Santa's workshop. I was in awe. It was magical.

Now this job had that same magic. I would be getting paid to write, to do what I love to do. With my shoulders back and head held high, I turned left and made my way to Human Resources for my first day of work.

Letter from Cindy Schultz—August 29, 1989

Dear Chrisy,

I just put Jacob on the school bus and I can't believe that next year Katie will be on the same bus, bound for kindergarten. She's looking forward to seeing all of her "best friends" in preschool again. We've been back-to-school shopping and she's up to a size 5. So far we've gotten all dresses and skirts and tights. That's our Katie.

Jacob has started to ask about babies in tummies and we've talked about how he was in Anastacia's tummy and Katie was in Chrisy's tummy and Jim was in my tummy. We just say that's the way it was meant to be.

One of Katie's favorite stories is when Dennis and I went to get her at the hospital when it was our turn to be her mom and dad. She also knows her teddy bear is a gift from you to her.

Katie is a great kid. Pink is still her favorite color and she loves things that are feminine and frilly. And she's so darned cute! Her vocabulary is incredible and she expresses herself very well. (You know when she's angry!)

Good luck with your new job! We always wish the best for you. Take care of yourself!

Love & hugs,
Cindy (and Dennis and kidlets)

CHAPTER 38

Spring 1990

You know you've truly arrived in your career—or at least you think so—when a package that requires immediate attention is being couriered to your apartment door on a Saturday afternoon.

After eagerly greeting the courier, I signed for the packages and ran my finger along the taped edges of the brown wrapping paper. Inside were the bluelines and keylines—the last stages of proofing before going to print—of the *Dayton Hudson Child-Care Handbook*. It was spring of 1990, and work-family balance and childcare issues were becoming the hottest buzzwords in corporate America. Dayton Hudson was already leading the bandwagon. Writing and managing the *Child-Care Handbook* was the biggest project I'd handled thus far in my young career, so I was nervous and excited to be getting the proofs.

I set the large, more than poster-sized pages on the carpeted floor and sat down to start my work. First, I began scrutinizing the black-and-white photographs of children. Extreme close-ups of bright eyes and big smiles adorned the pages. These were the faces of employees' children, from babies to toddlers, grade-schoolers to preteens. Black, white, Asian, American Indian—they were children of many nationalities, beautiful children, whose innocent, cherubic faces brought images of Katie to my mind.

My little girl was nearly five years old now, and it had been almost a year since I'd seen a picture of her. I wondered how she'd changed and grown over the past year and how she was faring in kindergarten.

I couldn't help but imagine her face here, on these pages. If I had kept her, her smiling face could sit on the pages of this publication.

Yes, I would have put her on the cover, and I would have said to everyone: "She's mine. Look at my daughter."

Guilt and sadness began to buzz slowly into my mind now. But I swatted at those feelings and kept knocking them away. My rational mind took over and I knew that if I had kept my baby girl, I wouldn't be here doing this today. I wouldn't have this job. I wouldn't be managing this project—she wouldn't be on the cover anyway. Katie was where she was supposed to be, and I was where I was supposed to be. I just had to keep telling myself that.

After circling a few imperfections in the photographs and scrutinizing the keylines for color breaks, I turned to the bluelines and began carefully proofing the words I'd written months earlier, words that would soon be printed and sent to employees.

Is my child safe? Did she eat a good lunch? Is she happy? These are questions you may often ask yourself while you're at work and your child is in day care. Even when you're assured that your child is safe and warm, your thoughts may turn to his or her well-being. It's often difficult to separate and balance your personal and professional life.

I found no typos. Just odd feelings knowing the questions that I asked myself about my child went so much deeper than questions about day care.

The phone rang, a welcome distraction. It was my boss, Lory. She wanted to come over and see the proofs. I'd appreciate the company, and the presence of another set of eyes would be a huge relief. I'd never proofed anything this big and important before. I didn't want to screw anything up.

When Lory arrived, she joined me on the living room floor of my small apartment, where we gushed about how great the handbook looked, how cute the pictures were (especially the one with her daughter), and how well it read. Gradually, after we agreed the book would be well received, our conversation turned with the pages, from business to personal.

"You know I'm adopted, right?" Lory asked. "Well, I've started my search to find my birth mother." The words "birth mother" hung in the air for several seconds, waiting for me to grab onto them. *Come on, talk,* they whispered.

"That's so wonderful, Lory. I bet your mom would love to see you."

"I know where I was born and have some other information, so I think I should be able to find her." I could see the excitement and anticipation in her eyes, hear the love and reverence in her voice, as she talked about a mother she didn't yet know.

"I'm sure she loved you very much. I should know because I'm a birth mom. I had a little girl five years ago."

There, the secret was out. I was happy to finally share my story with Lory. I told her about my Katie. I told her how much I loved my little girl, how cute and sweet she was, and how I hoped she would want to know me some day, like Lory wanted to know her own mother.

"I hope you find your mom. I bet she would love hearing from you and love you so much. And it would be such a big relief. I think about how hard it had to be back then, when it was so shameful and secretive. I feel bad for your mom and other women from that era."

We talked about the millions of women back then, well before open adoption, when giving a baby up was shrouded in secrecy and shame. There were millions of women who had given up their babies to anonymous parents, never knowing where and how their babies were.

I thought of these courageous women—often shunned by their families and communities—going through the discomfort of pregnancy and the pain of labor and childbirth, then having doctors and nurses whisk their babies away without being able to see or touch or kiss their own flesh and blood. I grieved for these women and prayed that they had found peace. I prayed for all the mothers who had placed their babies for adoption. We are members of a silent sisterhood, sharing a rite of passage that no one outside our circle could ever begin to understand.

A few months after that day sitting on the floor of my apartment, Lory found out who her birth mother was and where she had lived.

She also found out that her mother had died of breast cancer many years earlier, when her new baby daughter, Lory's half sister, was just one year old.

Lory was devastated. She would never meet the wonderful woman who gave her life thirty-some years ago. She and I grieved over this loss, over the fact that she would never know the woman who gave her life. She'd never be able to hug her, or ask her questions, or even lay eyes on the person whom she shared a body with. I also grieved for Lory's mother—that she didn't get the chance to know her amazing daughter, who was a wonderful, fun, loving human being and a mother herself.

Along with the sadness, I felt fear. Fear that the same thing could happen to Katie and me. What if I died before I had the chance to hold her again and before she had the chance to meet me? *Maybe I should go meet her.*

CHAPTER 39

June 1990

Joe, my new boyfriend, said he would love to meet my daughter someday. That was one of the things I loved about him right away—he embraced the fact that I had a daughter from the moment I told him. I also loved that he was fun, romantic, and an eternal optimist.

We were set up by Koleen, our mutual friend and coworker. Joe worked for Dayton's in the video-production department, which worked closely with my Internal Communications department. We both loved what we did, and we shared that passion. Both of our fathers had been entrepreneurs, so maybe that's where it came from. Or maybe it was that our careers involved our great loves—mine reading and writing, his watching movies and making videos.

We enjoyed movies and restaurants, walks around the lakes, art fairs, and happy hours. Joe was different from anyone I'd dated before, and he said the same about me. He said he liked that I was independent, interesting, smart, fun—and feisty. I'd gone out with many different types of guys. Way back in junior high, there were a few jocks. Then there were the partiers. In college, I dated Scott, who was my first boyfriend after Jim. Then, my senior year of college I dated a fellow *MSU Reporter* writer. After I moved to Minneapolis, I had just one date before I met Joe.

Joe was a charmer from the get-go, a gentleman at every turn. He opened doors for me—any and all doors—car doors, front doors, side doors. He held out my coat to help me put it on. He brought flowers to my door. He drove me to work and dropped me off at the front door, even though I really didn't mind taking the bus. It was sometimes over the top, but that was Joe.

I told Joe about Katie on our third date, over dinner at a Chinese restaurant. It was a big part of who I was and I wanted him to know. His response, when I'd finished my story, was: "That's so cool. That is a really great thing that you did."

That was so wonderful to hear. The men I dated since having Katie had acted like it wasn't a big deal. One even asked point-blank: "Well, why didn't you just have an abortion?" Just have an abortion, again, like it was no big deal. Maybe men just didn't and couldn't have any inkling of what a big deal it was—even though they could be fathers and parents, they could not be mothers. They would never know the sensation and power of having another human being living and growing inside them. They would never know the marvel of that final push that brings a new human being into the world.

"So do you ever want kids, at some point in your life?" I sensed the slight fear he had that perhaps I wasn't the motherly type, since I'd given a baby away.

"Oh, yeah. I do," I said. "Someday. Not for a long time, but someday."

Just four months after our first date, I took Joe home to Mitchell as my date for Becky's wedding. He made a great impression on everyone. People liked him. He was nice, polite, and funny—and what really got them was that he ironed.

It all started when someone asked: "Can you iron this shirt?" It was directed at me or my mom, or perhaps the women in general. "No, we can't iron! We're busy!" I responded. Plus, I wasn't very good at ironing. We girls were busy with hair and makeup and getting into our dresses and matching accessories.

"I can do it," Joe piped in with no prompting. He quickly set up his ironing station in the living room of 1007 Mitchell Boulevard and ironed a few pair of pants, some shirts, a tie. Whatever came his way, he did it with ease, a smile, and nice, straight creases.

This was a big deal at my house. I'd never caught any Bauer boys ironing when I was growing up. I'm not sure my brothers even knew how to turn the iron on. (Though the story goes that my dad was so picky about how his clothes were ironed when he was a young boy that he did it himself.) Our household chores growing up had been very traditional and segregated: the boys did outside work and manual labor, the girls did inside housework and cooking. That said, I have to admit I remember never having to do too much of anything. Could this be because I was the baby of the family? Or it was more likely that my mom spoiled all of us? Or maybe because we all had paying jobs starting at age fourteen.

Joe's honed domestic capabilities blew people away. And I have to say, I liked it too. It reinforced that he would be a good domestic partner, sharing household tasks and not thinking they were women's work.

"He's a keeper," more than one relative declared to me. I, too, had started thinking that perhaps he was a keeper. It became even more pronounced as we celebrated Becky and Bill's wedding day and the love of our family and friends.

Love was definitely in the air that day. I was feeling it, especially when I watched my sister walk down the aisle of Holy Spirit Catholic Church that warm, sunny July day. Becky looked so happy and beautiful as she walked arm in arm with my dad down the aisle. Her smile was radiant and beaming as she gazed back and forth across the aisles at her guests, smiling and nodding to those who'd come to celebrate.

I owed so much to this beautiful person. Other than my parents, she was the one who knew me the longest in this life, who knew me the best. We'd played dolls together in the darkness of our childhood bedroom and later fought over the space and cleanliness of the room. We grew apart for years, then came together when she welcomed me into her home and helped me through the toughest time in my life. She helped me bring Katie into the world and find a great home for her.

How can I ever repay you? I thought as I watched her and my dad approach the altar. But what she did for me couldn't ever be paid back. All I could do was love and support her and be the best friend that I could—and straighten the train of her dress to fulfill my duties as maid of honor.

Later that night, when it came time to catch Becky's bouquet, I didn't mess around. I stood at attention in the middle of the wooden dance floor, along with the dozen or so other women and girls—ages five to thirty-five—in a semicircle on the dance floor. Music played and anticipation built as we waited for Becky to get into bouquet-toss position.

I got into position too. My shoes were off, my drink was on the table, my adrenaline was pumping, and my hormones were raging. Becky turned around so her back was to us and did a little shimmy before yelling: "One, two, three," tossing the bouquet up over her head and into the air. As soon as the flowers left her fingers and launched into the air, I leapt like Superwoman flying through the crowd, over and between others, to grab the prized bouquet.

I got it. It was in my hand. It was fate. Or if not fate, at least it was an indicator that I was quick on my feet and determined.

"I got it," I yelled as I regained my balance and triumphantly held it up for all to see. I ran to Joe to kiss him. "I got it," I said again.

"I see that. And I hope to God no one is injured. You practically tackled all those other girls out there," he joked. "But I'm glad you got it."

CHAPTER 40

February 1991

Joe truly was glad I caught that bouquet, because seven months later on a trip to Florida, he asked me to marry him.

We had planned a getaway to Miami in mid-February. It was a perfect escape from the Minnesota cold and a chance for Joe to show me his old stomping grounds. He loved his alma mater, the University of Miami, and the better parts of the city, especially Coconut Grove. This seaside community was chock-full of great restaurants, bars, and shops, and we walked hand in hand along the docks and admired the boats and the seaside lifestyle.

Joe took me to the bars where he'd hung out during his college years, where he drank good, imported beer and ate oysters on the half shell. It was a huge contrast to where I'd attended college in south central Minnesota. Going to the "beach" when I was in college meant a small swimming pond on the outskirts of town. Our happy hour staple was nachos with orange, processed cheese, not fresh oysters on the half shell. Our beer of choice was definitely not imported; it was whatever was the cheapest, usually Old Milwaukee Light.

We decided to make our second evening in town a big night out with an expensive dinner. Joe picked a small, cozy restaurant and paid the maître d' well to get us a good table just feet from the open-air balcony. We savored wine, escargot, lobster, and steak. We held hands across the table between bites and soaked up each other and the warm sea air. It was romantic and wonderful.

After dinner, we strolled hand in hand along the palm tree–lined sidewalks of Coconut Grove. After a few blocks of walking, Joe flagged down one of the many rickshaw drivers on the street filled with young partygoers and couples.

"We want a ride to the water," Joe instructed the driver. We hopped in and got nestled in the cart, where we laughed and kissed as the driver pulled us along the streets of Coconut Grove toward the moonlit waterfront. Joe sat up as we got closer to the water and scanned the area. He ordered the driver to stop. "Right here; this is perfect," he said. The driver stopped and set the handles of the cart on the ground as Joe offered me his hand, gently leading me out of the cart onto the lush green grass.

And then I knew it was coming—the big "P." I was nervous and excited; happy and scared. This was it. He was going to propose. But oh, holy shit, I thought, we hadn't solved "the name thing."

The "name thing" disagreement flashed through my mind in the seconds that it took me to get out of the rickshaw and get my bearings. About two weeks before we left for Miami, we'd gotten into a heated argument about women keeping their maiden names (what is a maiden anyway?) when they got married. "I won't marry someone who won't take my last name," Joe boldly proclaimed that day as we drove down the freeway on the way to his apartment.

The statement made my hackles go up. I was always ready to defend my position, whatever it was. But I hesitated for a moment. I didn't want to regret any words that left my lips. But I also was always true to my heart, so I had to say it. My heart was pounding, but I had to stand my ground. I didn't want to lose Joe, but more than that I didn't want to lose myself. I was a feminist—I believed wholeheartedly that women are equal—and equality reaches to your name if you want it to. I felt that, if he really loved me, he'd understand. So I said it: "Well, I won't marry someone who doesn't respect the fact that I want to keep my name," I declared, and added, "So don't ask me."

The name thing was a deal breaker for me. I'd made up my mind while I was in college that I would keep my name. I'd had it all my life. I liked it. It was who I was—and I'd worked a long time to figure out who I was. I couldn't figure out why people didn't understand this. I was surprised that so many women changed their names. How could you be someone for twenty or thirty years and the next day be someone else? Why is a man's name more important than yours?

We drove the rest of the way home that night in silence. We talked about it briefly the next morning on our drive to work. I told Joe I was willing to break up over it. He didn't bring it up again.

As soon as I got my bearings, just a few feet from the rickshaw, Joe dropped to his knees—yes, just like in the movies—took my hand, and asked: "Christine Marie Bauer, will you marry me?"

Even though I had known something was up, I was still blown away by it. It was all so perfect; he was so sweet and wonderful, so romantic.

But holy shit! Am I really ready for this? I love Joe, for sure. But is he the right one? Is he really the one I'm meant to spend the rest of my life with? I don't know if I'm ready for this. Before I could think or question any longer, I just went with my gut. I responded: "Yes, I will marry you, Joseph Robert Schmelz."

He took my left hand and slid the gold band and diamond solitaire onto my finger. It was more than I'd ever imagined for a proposal. And a million times better than the first time around. We were both thrilled, and I figured we'd work "the name thing" out at some point, somehow.

Letter to Dennis and Cindy Schultz—December 19, 1993

Dear Dennis, Cindy, and Family,
Just in the nick of time I'm getting my Christmas cards and letters completed. This will be our first Christmas in our house, so we are very much looking forward to it. We are hosting our first official holiday dinner!

This first year in our house has gone very fast. It's amazing how much it takes to keep up a house! But finally, we feel like it's really home with all our personal touches. I think I told you about Wolfy, our big Samoyed. He's pretty cute, isn't he? And we love having him around. He's fun and so energetic—a little too energetic at times.

We've done quite a bit of traveling over the year. We went to New York City, Chicago, and Door County. I loved all the places. Door County was of course the most relaxing, and we hope to go back some day. In

February, we'll be going with my parents and Becky and Bill to Grand Cayman Island. I'm sure we'll love it.

Our jobs are going very well. I'm excited to start a new job in January. I'll be moving to the public relations department (I've been in the employee communications department), so it should be fun and challenging to work with the media.

What else? I was the cochair for a fundraising event for the Minnesota Literacy Council. We raised over $5,000 to help adults improve their reading and writing.

I think about Katie all the time and hope that she is having an easier time with reading. You said that she was having some trouble? Is she improving? I hope so. I would hate to have her get discouraged about school. I had some sort of visual processing problems when I was about her age too, and I went to some kind of therapy at the optometrist. I've been an avid reader and writer ever since.

Is Katie still involved with baton and soccer? I love to see pictures of her doing all the fun things she is involved in. She looks like she loves it. And I can tell that she is loved.

I seriously considered calling you a few months ago. I had an incredible urge to see Katie. Although my heart wants to, my head tells me it wouldn't be the best thing for Katie. Whenever she wants to see me, I'm ready. I see those pictures of the kids when you are in Minnesota and I daydream of running into you somewhere. I look forward to the day when I get to meet you in person and see Katie.

Having Becky and her baby Andrew around has been very fun. Joe and I are his godparents and we love him dearly. He's got Becky's personality and is a joy to have around. We only live a half hour away so we get to see them a lot.

As always, know that you are in my thoughts and prayers, especially Katie. I send my love. Please give her hugs and kisses for me. Please send some photos when you have a chance.

Love,
Chrisy

CHAPTER 41

Journal Entry—May 30, 1996

I dreamt last night that I woke up and wasn't pregnant anymore. I was very sad and confused. I'm sure that I dreamt it because yesterday was Katie's birthday. She's eleven years old. Unbelievable.

I just glanced through my journal from when I had her. How did I do it? I was so down on myself then; it was such a difficult time. But it's so different this time, of course. I love and hate being pregnant all at the same time. I still have nineteen weeks to go.

June 1996

When I felt the baby kick, it was like being knocked backward down a long, dark stairway through time. Though they were soft, fluttery kicks—like little butterflies—they packed a crushing emotional blow.

Because this was my second pregnancy, I recognized those little kicks right away—and I envisioned those tiny feet and little toes rubbing up against my uterus. But the joy and excitement that I felt for this new life inside me were pushed back by feelings of sorrow and loss for my firstborn.

I was on my way into work on a beautiful summer morning when these feelings all came rushing back to me with those tiny kicks. The soft flutters were like an electrical shock to my emotional system—the sensation jump-started my battery of despair.

Blinded by my tears and dizzy with anguish, I pulled my car over to the side of the road and gasped for air. As soon as I stopped the car and put it into park, it all came out—the grief, the anxiety, the fear, the joy, the pain. All of it. It came tumbling out of me in tears and sobs. I had given up my firstborn; eleven years later I was still grieving for her as the new little life was forming inside me, taking over the room in my belly that had once belonged to Katie.

When I could finally catch my breath, I called Joe from my cell phone. "Hi," is all I could muster with my wounded voice between breaths.

"Are you okay? What's going on?" Joe asked, with alarm ringing in his voice..

"Well, not really," I said with a deep sigh. "It's hard to explain, but I feel really, really sad. Like physically, I'm going through my pregnancy with Katie again, and I miss her then, and I don't know. It's just all messed up. This is supposed to be a happy time. We're having a baby."

It seemed like the right time to have a baby. We had been married for nearly five years and it felt right to start a family. There was also the fact that my clock had started ticking; I could hear it ringing loudly and clearly.

The closer I got to age thirty, the thought of having a baby became more than a want. It became a burning, innate desire to have a baby. It was primal, like the need to eat or drink or sleep. Physically, I craved a baby. After just a month of officially "trying," the need was filled.

"Do you need to come home? Want me to come get you?" I could tell Joe was ready to walk out the door to rescue me. He always liked the opportunity to be a rescuer—he liked to be a knight in shining armor.

The thought of him coming to get me and then going home and crawling into my bed was tempting. It would be so nice to lie in bed all day, weep when I felt like it, and sleep when I felt like it. But I wasn't one to lie around, certainly not one to miss work, unless I was very ill. My dad—who never missed a day of work in thirty years until he had his first heart attack—had instilled a strong work ethic in me.

"No, I think I'll be okay in a few minutes." I pulled the lever under the seat and tilted it back into a reclining position. I tried to relax while we talked. I had to pull it together.

We talked a while longer and agreed I should see a counselor to work through these complicated feelings. Just making that decision to seek counseling made me feel better; a sense of calm began to wash over me, at least enough to be able to go into work.

Within a week I was at my first counseling appointment at Children's Home Society, where they provided a range of services related to adoption. They were people who knew what I was going through. Over the next few meetings, the counselor and I talked about many of the delicate aspects of being a birth mother. Things like the awkwardness of the question I kept getting: "Is this your first?"

It came from people I knew and people I didn't, people at work or people in line at the grocery store, because being pregnant automatically means that you and the baby inside you are fodder for conversation.

We also discussed the fact that I hadn't ever talked much to my dad or my brothers about Katie. That bothered me. I tried a few times over the years to walk down that path, but they never wanted to go there. It was awkward with them. It was awkward for me.

We conversed about how I hadn't personally worked through all of my grief; I hadn't fully gone through all the stages. I know I had definitely gone through denial and anger, bargaining and depression. It was that final stage—the stage of acceptance—that kept eluding me. I'd gotten close to the acceptance stage, but instead of working through it and making that final big step eleven years ago, I buried it. I buried it deeply in the busyness of school, then the busyness of working at the newspaper, then the busyness of my career and Joe.

Keeping busy with school, a career, marriage, and a home was how I had coped with my feelings of loss and sadness. But the feelings wouldn't stay buried anymore. They kept crawling and digging their way back up to the surface, and now it was time to unearth them. It was time to dig them up, to bring them to the top, to see them and feel them and touch them and clean them up and set them free.

Among many other things, my counselor told me that when I started crying, I shouldn't hold it in. I shouldn't try to stop it. Instead, I needed to let it out and breathe. Cry and breathe. Let go of the guilt. Let it go. I'd done nothing wrong. I'd done everything right. I'd done something good. I was a birth mom and had made someone else a mom. I was good.

In order to get ready to have my second baby, I would need to deal with those intimate and intense feelings that stemmed from the first.

September 9, 1996

Dear Chrisy,
First things first: CONGRATULATIONS to you and Joe on your upcoming little bundle of joy. We're so happy for you both. I hope all your thoughts on pregnancy are positive and that your memories of your past pregnancy can transfer now, eleven years later, as all positive. It's wonderful.

Our son Jake's birth mom lives in California now, and she kept in touch with us for about two years after Jake was born. She did not contact us for many years, and then, about four years ago, we got a phone call from her just to talk. She had gotten married and had a ten-month-old daughter. She was very excited about motherhood, but there was also a part of her that was nostalgic over what she had missed out on with Jacob. We got her updated on Jacob—she felt much better after that and said she could now go on without "Jake's ghost" hanging around, as she put it. We got a Christmas card with pictures from her that year and haven't heard from her since.

I'm only telling you this to let you know how another birth mom handled getting married and having a baby. How it brought back all kinds of feelings and emotions. Please always know that any letters or calls are welcome. If there is anything we can help you with, please let us know . . .

Lots of love,
Cindy and Dennis and Katie (good luck!)

CHAPTER 42

October 10, 1996

"She's in the bathroom?!" the nurse asked in disbelief. I could hear the alarm in her voice through the bathroom door as she talked to Joe out in the hallway. "She shouldn't be in the bathroom when her contractions are a minute apart."

As soon as I emerged, the nurse pushed the wheelchair up behind me and ordered me to sit down. "I don't mind walking," I responded casually—it was all seeming so easy—but she made me take the ride.

She quickly wheeled me into a room that was rather plain, not like the nice labor and delivery rooms they had shown us on the hospital tour months earlier. It seemed like a regular old room, and it was. They were busy and needed to get me in a room now, she explained, and then instructed me to get into my hospital gown and into bed pronto so she could check me.

"What do you mean no time for an epidural?" I said incredulously when she told me I was dilated to seven centimeters already and there was no time for that. "But it's in my birth plan, and I've talked to my doctor about it. I want one. I've had one before."

I thought so much would be like it had been before—at least the physical part. That I would go to the hospital, get comfy in my deluxe room, have an epidural, and kick back until it was time to push. I was wrong.

"It won't be long until you're ready to start pushing. There is absolutely no time for an epidural. That would have had to take place a few hours ago."

"But I've only been having contractions for a few hours," I explained.

Luckily, I had listened to Joe, who insisted on us leaving for the hospital when we did. I'd wanted to stay home, take a bath, and maybe watch a little more must-see Thursday night TV—my contractions started during *Seinfeld*. I'd even started running the bathwater when Joe insisted I gather my things and get in the car.

"You're lucky it's so fast," said the nurse. I was indeed lucky. Labor and delivery were easy, relatively speaking, if you consider it's like pushing a watermelon out of your vagina.

Less than an hour after getting to the hospital, it was time for me to push. I'd never seen the doctor before and would never see him again. He was simply the guy who happened to be on duty. He came in to essentially catch the baby and get the glory. "Okay, time for you to push," he said simply after a very brief introduction.

With only a few painful pushes—truly less than a handful—I felt the baby slide out of me, and then a tremendous sense of relief as this precious being made its debut into the world.

"It's a boy!" the doctor said. With those three words, he held up our tiny, perfect, 6.8-ounce little boy in his hands and turned him toward me.

Joy, relief, and amazement washed over me. I had done it again. I'd brought a healthy new life into the world. I stared at my little boy, and I thanked God for him. I told myself to seal this image in my mind. I wanted to hold forever this instant of my baby boy being presented to me and the world for the very first time, just like I could remember so vividly the feeling of holding Katie for the first time. It was etched in my arms and mind and heart forever. It had worried me that once I had my second baby, I wouldn't remember my first experience as well or would somehow forget it altogether. But my counselor assured me that I would not forget. Instead, I would create a new, special memory when I had my next baby, and I did. Right then and there, I did. I would embrace and treasure each one.

"We have our Dylan, honey," Joe said, beaming with pride over his baby boy, whose name we first happened upon in a TV show. We liked it not only because of how it sounded but because it meant "son of the sea," which seemed both powerful and gentle. And there was the cool factor that came from literary and edgy namesakes Dylan Thomas and Bob Dylan.

"Oh, yes we do," I replied as I reached out to touch him. "Oh, he's amazing; he's so beautiful," I whispered.

Joe gladly accepted the offer from the doctor to cut the cord. Then they laid this beautiful little babe on my tummy. Joe came to my side and we gazed down at him together. Dylan whimpered ever so slightly and then was quiet and calm, serene.

"We have a little boy," I repeated in wonder as I touched his tiny hands and peered into his dark, blinking eyes, eyes that were staring at me and struggling to adjust to the brightness of the world. He looked directly into my eyes for just a minute and stole my heart forever.

Two days later, on my thirty-first birthday, we brought Dylan home. We were released from the hospital on a glorious, sunny October day, and I took it all in—the warmth and the sunshine, this bundle of love in my arms, and my mom and Joe at my sides. What an incredible birthday gift I had in my hands and all around me.

When I looked at my mother, I remembered my birthday twelve years earlier—my nineteenth birthday—when I'd told her I was pregnant. When I wasn't ready to be a mom and thought maybe I never would be ready. I thought then that I'd never be happy again. So much had happened since then. So many good things had happened.

Baby Dylan made being a new mom fairly easy for me. *Easy* is a relative term. You can read all the pregnancy and baby books that you want, but nothing can totally prepare you for the all-consuming nature of this job and the sheer exhaustion that comes with it. He was an uncomplicated, mellow baby, which was increasingly evident as the hours, days, and weeks went by. At just five days old, he slept five hours straight, and he hardly ever cried, other than when he was hungry or just waking up. He was a dream baby.

Dylan's demeanor was a huge relief, since I had worried so much during my pregnancy that all of my tears and sadness might impact him. I'd worried that he would be emotionally traumatized from hearing and sensing all that crying when he was in the womb. I'd worried about that with Katie, too.

But that wasn't the case at all. It seemed the opposite had happened. Dylan was an incredibly happy and easygoing baby. From what Cindy told me, Katie had been too. Maybe it was because I'd done enough crying for all of us before; now it was time for everyone to be happy.

Journal Entry—October 30, 1996

I'm looking at my beautiful son Dylan, watching him sleep. His innocence and peacefulness amaze me now as they do every day. So do his beauty and perfection and the way he looks at me. It's all such a miracle.

Dylan Bauer Schmelz will be three weeks old tomorrow evening at 11:24 p.m. The whole labor and delivery are still kind of a blur since things happened so fast. It was really a breeze in comparison to others I hear about. Three hours from start to finish. I can't really vividly remember him being on my tummy right away after he was born, although I vividly remember seeing him when they held him up; I said "He's got his daddy's nose" and thought he was the most beautiful thing I'd ever seen.

I had thought about how I'd feel that first instant so much because I remember what it was like to hold Katie in my arms—so warm in her blanket. I worried too that I might feel sadness when Dylan came, but I didn't. I just felt total joy and amazement. I love little Dylan with every fiber and cell of my body. I've cried quite a few times when I've held him, afraid that something might happen to him. I've cried too for Katie, hoping that life is being good to my little girl and praying that nothing bad will ever happen to her. Dylan is awake now, his huge, blue eyes looking at me.

CHAPTER 43

April 1999

The sound was horrible—a dull, heavy *thud*.

It was the sound of a little skull hitting cement tile at full force. Blood was squirting everywhere.

"Oh my God. Oh my God. Dylan!" I screamed and ran to my little boy, who a split second before had been laughing and running at full speed, until he tripped and came crashing into the step right before my eyes. I watched it happen, and there was nothing I could do.

I leapt toward him, picked him up, and attempted to comfort him, while I myself was on the verge of hysteria. On instinct, I set myself in motion. I quickly grabbed a dish towel out of the kitchen drawer and within seconds ran out the front door toward my neighbor's house. My thought was that I needed someone to take us to the hospital quickly. I had to save my baby.

"It's going to be okay, it's going to be okay," I repeated to Dylan as I ran in a frenzy down the driveway and out onto the street.

We were halfway across when two-year-old Dylan, held tightly against my chest, said: "It's okay, Mommy. Don't cry, Mommy. I want to go home."

I stopped in my tracks. *Okay, calm down. Listen to your kid. Get it together.*

"Oh my God. You're okay! Let Mommy see," I pulled the towel back and got a better glance at the large goose egg forming on his head. A deep, inch-long gash ran down the center of it, just above and between his huge blue eyes. Pieces of his blonde hair were stuck in the blood.

I laughed nervously at just how crazy it was that my two-year-old was telling *me* not to cry as blood trickled down his face. It was a nasty gash, no doubt, a major owie, but it was not life-threatening. He would survive.

I took a deep breath and turned back toward home. "I'm glad you are okay, honey," I told him as reassuringly as I could. "I was just crying because I was worried and I felt bad that you got hurt. You're going to be just fine."

"I know, Mommy. I'll be fine," he assured me.

My thoughts turned to Katie for a few minutes as I wondered if she'd had any injuries that had resulted in lots of blood. Cindy had never mentioned that, but that didn't mean it hadn't happened. I'd never know all of the details and milestones of her life. But if she had some big injury, she was certainly in good hands. It was comforting to know that Dennis was a doctor and would know just what to do in an emergency, that he'd remain calm.

At that point, I made a note to myself for now and the future: *You must stay calm. You are the mom.* I also made a note that something like this could likely happen again; I needed to buck up and be prepared. Dylan was a very active little boy, running, jumping, climbing, and falling all the time. My mom liked to say: "Dylan went from crawling to running. He never bothered to walk." She was right. He was always on the go, going fast. He made me tired.

Back in the house, I cleaned the wound as best I could, got an icepack, and picked up the phone to call Becky. I always called Becky. I called her when I needed mothering advice or assistance. I called Becky when I needed an ear to listen or a shoulder to cry on. I called Becky when I needed someone to laugh with me. I don't know what I'd do without Becky.

Becky was my very own, living, breathing, talking parenting book. She was always reading the latest parenting books, whereas I'd only read *What to Expect from Your Newborn* and *What to Expect the First Year*. I'd purchased *What to Expect in the Toddler Years*, but hadn't read it much. Between working and chasing Dylan, I just didn't have the time. I'd try to read when I went to bed, but I'd make it through only a few paragraphs and then would crash from exhaustion. Oh well, those books probably didn't say anything about head wounds anyway.

"Hi, Beck. We've got an injury here and I think we need stitches. I'm wondering if you can drive me to the urgent care. Joe's at work."

I described the wound in more detail and she agreed stitches were likely in order. So in fifteen minutes, my sweet sister was there to help me out. By that time Dylan was running around the house, playing with his toys, and excited to see his cousin, Ali.

Ali, Becky's little girl, was just six weeks older than Dylan, and they were best buddies. Once we arrived at urgent care, the two of them ran around the waiting room having fun, without a care in the world. Dylan seemed to forget that he had a gaping wound in the middle of his forehead. Ah, to be so carefree.

Dylan was having loads of fun until they called us back to the exam room and confirmed the need for stitches—and the need to strap him to the table so he wouldn't move during the procedure.

It was awful for him and awful for me, but I didn't cry this time. I had to be brave for Dylan as he wiggled and writhed under the straps that held his little body to the table. My heart ached as I watched, and I wished it could be me lying there instead of him.

He made it through the procedure just fine, though, and when he was done, he was quite proud of the battle wound on his head. "Looks like a dead fly," he said, touching the stitches gently as he looked in the mirror.

"You were so brave," I told him. "You were brave at the doctor and at home. You were braver than me! Here Mommy was running and crying and you had to tell me everything was all right."

I turned to Becky. "Seriously, Becky, he had to tell *me* to stop crying. And I could have driven us here myself, rather than bothering you. God, what is wrong with me? Talk about being a hysterical mom. I need to be calmer in these situations."

Becky reminded me of what was wrong: "Chrisy, you are pregnant and your hormones are raging. That's normal."

"Oh, yeah, that probably had something to do with it." I was going to be a mom again.

CHAPTER 44

October 1999

There is love. And then there is mother love. It is that pure, raw, unconditional, automatic, from-every-fiber-of-your-being love.

It's the love that jolts you out of a dead sleep in the middle of the night, even though the baby is making only a faint whimper (and your husband can't hear it at all).

It's the love that makes you laugh, even when you're getting peed on, pooped on, and spit-up on right when you're ready to walk out the door to go to work.

It's the love that makes you continue breastfeeding even though you have a fever of 102 and your breasts are as hard as concrete, three times their normal size, and sore as hell because of an infection.

It's the love that would make you not hesitate to rip someone's throat out if they hurt your precious baby.

It's the love that makes you do whatever you need to do for this little being that is helpless without you, even though you are so tired you can hardly stand up.

It's the love that brings you to the brink of tears and then makes you burst out laughing. It's the best kind of love.

"Mommy, let me in," Dylan said as he pounded on the bathroom door. "I want in."

"Just a minute, honey, I'm going potty," I yelled through the bathroom door to my very active and precocious three-year-old. "It's mommy's turn to go poopy"—or at least try—and oh, what I'd give for a few quiet minutes in the bathroom by myself.

Instead, I had a two-week-old baby in his bouncy seat lying in front of me and a three-year-old pounding on the door as I attempted to relieve myself. I'd brought the baby into the bathroom to protect him from his big brother. Dylan loved his new brother, Jared. He loved him so much that he wanted to touch him, hold him, and hug him every minute. So much so that I eventually resorted to putting a latch high up on the outside of Jared's bedroom door so that Dylan couldn't get in and climb into his crib.

"Mommy. Let me *innnnn*." Dylan kept pounding, and then Jared started crying. Loud. Jagged. Desperate cries.

I couldn't resist any longer. I reached forward, opened the door, peeked out at Dylan, and then bent down to pick up Jared.

Dylan pushed open the door and walked in. He was thrilled—mission accomplished. He'd made it. He stood just inches in front of me, smiling, awaiting attention as I sat on the toilet, holding a crying baby.

Oh, how I desperately wanted just a few minutes to myself. I was near tears, so near tears. I was going to lose it. I just wanted a few minutes to myself to go to the bathroom. But oh no, no I wouldn't let myself cry. I couldn't. I was the mom. So instead, I laughed. Big, deep belly laughs. Pee your pants kind of laughs, so it was very convenient that I was sitting on the toilet.

"What is so funny, Mommy? How come you are laughing, Mommy?" Dylan said as he stood inches from me and touched my face (and of course, Jared's face).

"Because you and your brother are so cute, and I love you so much," I said over Jared's cries. "I love you so much."

Dylan's brother—Jared Bauer Schmelz—arrived three weeks shy of Dylan's third birthday. The pregnancy with Jared was wonderful. I fully enjoyed being pregnant this time, finally. And with the exception of some preterm labor, which got me two much-needed weeks of bed rest, everything went very smoothly. Although Dylan wanted desperately to name his brother "Strawberry Banana," we decided instead to call him Jared, which means "perpetual leader."

"Come on, let's play, Mommy," Dylan said as Jared continued to cry.

Jared stopped crying for just a second, replacing his cry with a grunt. I heard the gushing sound and felt the warmth of it in his diaper. "Yes, we'll play in a minute, honey. First you can help me change Jared's diaper."

Dylan was thrilled. He loved to help with the baby. We made our way out of the small bathroom and went to Jared's room to put on a clean diaper.

I watched both of the boys in awe as Jared lay naked on his changing table and Dylan stood on his little chair right next to him, gently touching his brother's cheeks and nose. He got up close, cheek to cheek, and said: "Hi, Jared. Hi, little brother. You are *so* cute."

As I watched this beautiful display of love and wonder, baby Katie crawled into my mind. I vividly envisioned the pictures Cindy had sent me over the years, especially the one from her first day home from the hospital. Katie was lying on a changing table, swaddled in a blanket, with big brother Jake hovering over her, smiling at her, touching her, just exactly like Dylan was doing right now to Jared.

I thought of the many other pictures Cindy had sent me over the years that were now in a photo album along with all the letters. I had photos of baby Katie in the bathtub. Katie as a toddler emptying the dishwasher. Katie with spaghetti all over her face and hair. I smiled thinking about how much Dylan looked like his big sister when she was little. Fuzzy blonde hair, big blue eyes, heart-shaped lips, perfectly placed dimples.

There were also many pictures of the firsts: the first days of school, first lost tooth, and first Christmas, as well as getting her ears pierced, soccer games, dance recitals, and choir concerts. There were so many missed moments and milestones. Thinking of them all made my heart ache, but at the same time I was grateful that Cindy had shared so many of these moments with me. I got to watch her grow up, even if it was from hundreds of miles away.

I also had pictures of Katie and her three siblings in Chicago with skyscrapers in the background; pictures of her and her siblings hiking in the mountains of Utah; snapshots of her at Disney World in front of the entrance to the Magic Kingdom. There were photos of her smiling and holding a baby alligator while on a swamp tour in New Orleans, and amongst the seashells on the beaches of Padre Island.

I knew she was having a good life and that she was with the right family. As I watched Dylan hovering over Jared, I was hopeful that someday she would be part of this family too, that someday I would add to her photo album a picture of her smiling and laughing with her brothers.

CHAPTER 45

June 2001
I recognized Cindy's handwriting as soon as I pulled the envelope out of the mailbox. It was very distinct, with big block letters, and the right corner of the envelope held extra postage for the pictures I could feel inside. It was always such a treat to hear from her and get a report on Katie, especially now; my girl had turned sixteen last month.

Cindy's letters and pictures provided glimpses into my daughter's life, snapshots of her well-being and happiness. I tucked the other mail under my arm so I could hold this letter with both hands. I paused and then squeezed it, confirming the treasures it held within—words and pictures of my daughter's life.

Whenever I received a letter from Cindy, I'd savor it in my hands a bit before opening. It was special and to be revered. I'd make sure I was by myself and that the room was quiet before I gently tore open the envelope and devoured its contents. It was easier to do that on this particular day because I was working from home—the boys were at day care and Joe was at work. I didn't have to wait. I rushed inside, sat down on the couch, opened the letter, and began reading.

May 30, 2001

Dear Chrisy,
Where to begin with our fabulous Katie . . . she is turning out to be a wonderful, wonderful person. As I think back over the past year and try to think of the highlights there are so many that I don't know where to begin, so I'll go chronologically.

One of the main things that come to mind for our girl is her faith. Last year Katie was confirmed and for the first time in our church's history she went to our pastors (a wonderful husband and wife team) and asked if she could plan a church service, including writing and delivering the sermon. Pastors Tom and Debbie were so excited about her request and were more than happy to help her with this.

Last March, she actually got up in front of the congregation and led the entire church service, including the sermon. There wasn't a dry eye in the house as she finished her sermon about tolerance and love. People just sat there with their mouths open that such wisdom could come from one so young. We were so proud of her!!!

Katie was also in the play and the musical last year. She got her first letter for her letter jacket in drama and music. She has a beautiful singing voice. . . . Also, this spring she got inducted into the National Honor Society. Yes, our precious Katie has a 3.8 GPA!! Once again we are so proud of her. It's hard to think that she tested in the 17th percentile in second grade and we had her going to Alverno College for summer school for two summers. She was just a late bloomer. Her teachers love her as she is always willing to go the extra mile and always has her homework done on time and correctly. I'm sure she's a breath of fresh air at the high school level . . .

Can you believe our girl turned sixteen yesterday? She got her temporary license last week so now she wants to drive us everywhere. As part of her birthday present, Dennis let her drive on the freeway last night before dark. She was so excited. (I was so nervous I couldn't go along.)

Also, Katie told me that for her eighteenth birthday she wants to go to Minneapolis for the chance to meet you.

As soon as I read those words, I cried out in joy and shock. I stood up and then quickly dropped to my knees. It was an instantaneous reflex. I crumbled with emotion. What I'd hoped and prayed for since I let her go sixteen years ago was going to happen. I would get to see and hold her again. She wanted to meet me.

I knelt there on the floor, clutching the letter in my hand while I soaked it in, and then read the rest of the words that were like a rope, tethering us together.

We are always teasing each other about how I will go with her and wait back at the motel room, but she says she wants to go on her own. We've got time to work out the logistics, but this is a heads-up that she really wants this for her eighteenth birthday. We have no problem with this. She has been such a precious gift to us.

She made it through her "turbulent adolescence" just fine and came out of it a really great kid who's fun to be with. Right now her biggest problem in life is that she has a haircut appointment next week and she can't decide how short to get her hair cut. We have numerous hairstyling magazines around the house right now and many of her friends are going with short hair, so we are entering a crisis phase right now. (Oh, to be young again.)

CHAPTER 46

June 2002

I quit the job that they paid and respected me for—account supervisor at the PR firm Padilla Speer Beardsley—and went full time with the job that they loved me for: Mommy.

Dylan was five years old and going to be entering kindergarten in the fall; Jared would be three and ready for preschool. My babies were growing up and I felt time was passing too quickly; I wanted to spend all the time that I could with them.

I wanted nothing more that summer than to be with them every minute of every day. I wanted to hold them and hug them as long as I wanted—or as long as they wanted me to—in the morning without having to rush out the door. I wanted to lie on the floor and play cars and trucks and Legos without worrying about what time it was and what I needed to get done next. I wanted to spend lazy days at the pool, the park, and the zoo, to walk barefoot with them in the backyard for hours at a time.

For a long time, I'd wanted to stay at home, but it hadn't really been possible for financial reasons. I also had a hard time admitting it to myself—after all, I'd been a very career-minded girl. I loved what I did. But I loved being a mom more than anything. Joe's business taking off in a new trajectory had made it possible, and we decided I could make the leap. Joe's travel schedule also heavily impacted the decision. His new projects and clients were taking him on the road and all over the world for weeks at a time.

It was on one of his twelve-day trips that I decided to throw in the towel. I was juggling client demands as well as the demands of caring for two active boys; a large, high-maintenance dog; and the household tasks and chores. I felt that at any moment the balls were going to start dropping, and I was having my own internal mommy wars.

For our first day of weekday freedom, Dylan, Jared, and I put on our swimsuits, packed our beach bag, and went to the community center swimming pool, where we met Becky, Andrew, and Ali. I was on top of the world. Instead of sitting in an air-conditioned meeting room or in front of a computer screen, I was on a lawn chair soaking in the sun and slathering sunscreen on two squirming, jumping little bodies.

I watched the other moms that day and wondered if they were appreciating this precious time they had with their kids as much as I was. It was hard work to be home with kids all day, no doubt about that, but at this point in my life, this felt like the most precious gift in the world to me.

Sitting on the warm cement at the edge of the pool with my legs dangling in the cool water, I vacillated between joining in and just watching these two beautiful little people of mine—Dylan with his blonde hair, huge blue eyes, and milky-white skin, and Jared with his brown hair, big brown eyes, and honey-colored skin. I admired their bulging little bellies, their curved little backs, and their round, firm little bottoms as they laughed and splashed each other. They were perfect little specimens of life.

I delighted in their awe and wonder at the water that sprayed up from the ground, at their laughter at the thrill of riding down the small water slide. We melted with love as their warm bodies dissolved in my arms, drifting slowly in circles around the lazy river.

Leaning back on the water floatie, I tilted my head back and let the sunshine warm my face and my boys warm my heart. I was so thankful for the opportunity to do this, to be home with my boys. I'd missed a whole childhood of this with my girl.

For several mornings that first week of being home and periodically over the summer, the boys would ask: "Are you going to work, Mama?"

"Nope," I replied happily. "I'm hanging out with you all day and night. Lucky me!"

"Yay," they'd cheer and jump up and down. So would I.

I'd also loved my jobs, but I knew there would always be clients to help, meetings to attend, press releases and annual reports to write, stories to craft, and reporters to pitch. But my boys would never again be five and two.

I was where I was supposed to be, and I transitioned easily as my weekdays went from being busy with my clients and meetings to being busy trying to convince my children to eat their vegetables; from eating lunch at the latest hot spot in downtown Minneapolis to eating peanut butter and jelly sandwiches at the bench in the park. I wouldn't have traded it for anything in the world.

Out of habit for much of the summer, I kept looking down at my wrist to check the time, but there was no watch there. I vowed not to wear it all summer. I'd spent the past six years constantly looking at my watch and living my work day in fifteen-minute increments because that was how I billed my time. Not anymore. My time was now measured and valued not by billable minutes but rather by laughter, smiles, tears, trips to the bathroom, trips to the park, and more.

Email from Cindy Schultz—March 30, 2003

I thought I'd better drop a line and let you know we are all well. Katie wants to write you a letter so badly and has two of them all set to go, but she just isn't satisfied with what they say and hasn't mailed anything so I thought I'd better "sneak" off an email to you.

She was so excited and nervous to get your letter. She really is looking forward to seeing you, but she will occasionally say, "I just don't know how to feel about all of this!" She says it in a good way, she's just so happy about all of it!

I don't know how much to tell you, as I'm sure Katie wants to tell you herself, but I'll fill you in on some of the upcoming events. Graduation is Sunday, June 8, and around June 14, Katie will take off for three weeks to go to Germany for a class trip. They were supposed to go last year and it was canceled. She is excited to go and will stay with the girl that was with us for three weeks last September. She gets back July 5 and will then be in Minneapolis for a church conference the weekend of July 11. The conference ends July 15 and then she'll be at UW–Eau Claire July 18 for a Leadership Conference.

YIKES, that's quite the schedule!!! She is one of the youngest delegates representing the SE Wisconsin Conference for our church. Also, as you can tell, she has chosen to go to UW–Eau Claire and will, so far, major in journalism. Sometime in there we will get the BIG REUNION planned. I'm putting the ball in Katie's court and letting her figure out when she wants to do this. I don't want to overwhelm her.

She is still a GREAT KID. Her smile literally lights up the room . . . This weekend is musical weekend again, and FHS is doing Grease. Katie plays the principal and once again lights up the stage.

That's about all from here. I just wanted to let you know that things are on track for the BIG REUNION. Katie just wants it all to be perfect. She is such a fabulous kid I can't even put it into words. YOU WILL LOVE HER, EVEN BEYOND BLOOD TIES!!!!!! It gives me shivers to think that we are ALL part of God's most-excellent plans for us on Earth. AREN'T WE LUCKY?!?! THANK YOU, THANK YOU for making it all possible . . .

Love to you and your family,
We'll see you soon! (Has a nice ring to it, don't you think?)
Cindy (and Katie)

Finally, after eighteen years, it was going to happen. I was going to hold my baby again. It was what I had been hoping and praying for all these years. It had been over six thousand days since I'd last touched her and held her and told her I loved her. I wondered how many times I'd thought of her during this time—a million? Or more? Even if I wasn't thinking of her consciously, she was always there in my subconscious, in my heart, in my soul.

What will it be like to meet? I remember her, but she doesn't remember me. Will she love me right away? Will she even like me right away? Oh, I hope so. I think so, but this is big. This is huge. I was excited and nervous at the same time, but mostly, I was just so happy.

CHAPTER 47

May 2003
Katie's eighteenth birthday was approaching and I wanted to get her something special. Becky came up with the idea of a charm bracelet made especially for her.

So together Becky and I went to her jewelry-maker friend and carefully selected each charm that would make up the bracelet: a heart that said "faith, hope, love," symbolizing my love for her and the faith and hope we had for reuniting; a cross to represent her faith; a "2003" to symbolize both her graduation year and the year we would meet; a musical note for her love of music; and birthstones for the birth months of Katie and her two mothers. It was perfect.

I sent it via priority mail so that it would arrive on her birthday, May 29. And then I held my breath waiting for her call or an email saying she got it. After several days of fretting over why she had not yet called me, I realized that she must be out of town. She would have called.

Then, finally, I heard.

From: Katie Schultz
To: Chris Bauer
Sent: Thursday, June 5, 2003, 10:44 p.m.
Subject: Thank you with all my heart

Chrisy,
Words cannot express how truly touched I am at receiving the charm bracelet for my eighteenth birthday. It is so extremely beautiful. Each charm means so much to me, especially knowing that you put it together.

I have worn it every day this week and think of you fondly when I wear it. All of my friends have been asking me where I got such a beautiful bracelet and I tell them it's from someone who loves me very much. It is the second greatest gift I've ever received; the first greatest gift being your love.

I'm so sorry that it has taken me a while to write back. Things have been very hectic around here. I've been preparing for exams and preparing for leaving high school. It is all so surreal to me. I can't believe today was my last day of high school. It all went by so fast. Today we had a rehearsal for the graduation ceremony and a friend and I had to sing the national anthem to practice. I was so nervous, but we sang it well. I was clutching my charm bracelet the whole time for good luck. I know it will bring me luck when I sing on Sunday.

It's also hard to believe I will be leaving for Germany a week from Sunday. When the German students were here in the fall, we all became very good friends. It will be wonderful to see them again. I just can't believe I'll be away from home for three weeks. I've never been away from home for that long or in a place that doesn't speak English. I'm sure I will have a wonderful time, or at least I hope so.

I know that Dylan and Jared will have a wonderful summer because they've got such a cool mom to hang out with. I am looking forward to meeting you this summer and giving you a gigantic hug. Maybe before I go to Germany we can give each other a call? I would love to hear your voice. I've tried for so long to imagine what it sounds like. I hope that you are doing well. Say hello to everyone for me. Thanks again for the absolutely beautiful gift. It is so precious to me.

Love always,
Katie

I smiled from ear to ear as I read the email again and again and again. And I couldn't wait for more.

From: Katie Schultz
To: Chris Bauer
Sent: Thursday, July 24, 2003, 1:59 PM
Subject: Hi other mother!

Hi Chrisy,
I have just returned home from an amazing "world"-wind summer. Germany was wonderful. I have so many amazing stories to tell you! My stay in Minnesota for General Synod was wonderful also, and Eau Claire was great, too. I have been waiting my whole summer and my whole life to meet you and that day is getting closer! I hope your summer is going well and that moving is going along smoothly. Let me know how things are looking on your end for coming up with a meeting date. I can't wait to hear from you again!!

   Love always,
   Katie

"Katie called me her 'other mother,'" I yelled to Joe over my shoulder, giddy with excitement. "Look at this, here in the subject line," I said, touching the words on the computer screen.

He peeked over my shoulder to read the email. "That's really cool," he said. "I can't wait to meet her."

We wouldn't have to wait long at all. The Big Day was set for August 16, 2003, and the plan was for Katie to come to our home and stay for a few days. Katie had gone back and forth as to whether or not she'd have Cindy come with her or if she would come by herself. In the end, she chose to come by herself—incredibly courageous for an eighteen-year-old.

CHAPTER 48

August 16, 2003

The ring of the doorbell made me jump, interrupting my flurry of activity. I was running in circles, cleaning, cooking, setting the table, attempting to make everything perfect for the arrival of my little girl.

"Is she here? Is that her?" Dylan asked as he and Jared flew toward the door. At ages seven and four, they were fast and they were excited. They couldn't wait to meet their big sister. They loved the idea of having a sister and were at that beautiful stage of life where acceptance is easy and effortless and hearts and minds are wide open.

They didn't have many questions about why I put her up for adoption or why she didn't live with us; they really didn't understand or care about those details. They were just excited to have a big sister. "No, it's too early for Katie, guys," I said as I walked to the door, hoping I was right—I wasn't quite ready.

"It's someone with flowers," said Dylan as he peeked out the window. "Should I let them in?"

"Sure, open the door," I said. As soon as he did, we saw the beautiful bouquet of flowers complete with a pink "It's a Girl" balloon.

"How cute!" I said as I took the flowers, set them on the dining room table, and grabbed the card from its holder. It read:

"Congratulation on your new arrival. We're thinking of you. Have fun. We love you! Dennis and Cindy."

They were simply amazing. Of all the people in the world, I had picked the best parents—or the best had been brought to me.

"Who gave you those?" Dylan asked as his nimble little fingers touched the flowers, the balloon, and everything else within reach.

"They're from Katie's other mommy and daddy. That is so sweet."

"Cool." Then, for the tenth time: "When is she going to get here?"

Pacing back and forth from room to room, I could hardly wait for her either. Soon I'd be holding my little girl again. The thought of her triggered my memory of holding her for the first time; I could still feel her in my arms.

As it got closer to Katie's arrival time, Joe got ready with the video camera. He and the boys followed me around and around as I paced and wandered. Each time I passed the dining room table, I smiled at the bouquet.

From the dining room window, I saw a car drive by slowly and pause in front of our house. It had to be her. She headed down to the end of the cul-de-sac to turn around.

"She's here. She's here, guys," I shouted to the boys. "Oh my God. Oh my God. She's here." I turned in circles and flapped my hands, trying to shake the nervousness out of me. The moment that I'd been waiting for half my life was finally here.

As soon as her maroon Ford Taurus pulled up at the curb, I ran out the door to greet her. She stepped out of the car just as I walked up to her, this beautiful, poised young lady.

"You're taller than me!" I said as I put my arms around her and held her tight. Then I felt a bit stupid that it was the first thing I said. "Oh my God, it feels so good to hold you and to hug you," I said, relishing her presence in my arms again.

We stood in the street hugging, tears streaming down our faces. It was surreal to be standing face-to-face, seeing, touching, and holding my own flesh and blood whom I'd held so briefly and let go of so achingly eighteen years ago. It was an intensely beautiful and powerful moment, as well as an anxious one. *Does she love me or hate me for what I did? Will she ever know just how much I love her? How will she like her little brothers? Will she fit in with us? Will it be awkward? What if she visits and then that's it, she doesn't want to see us anymore?*

The range and depth of my emotions were overwhelming. I imagined it must be the same or more for Katie, a mere eighteen, meeting her birth mother and relatives. *Okay. Buck up and be the mom here. Deep breaths. Take deep breaths and take charge,* I told myself.

"Let's go meet your brothers." Joe and the boys were in the

driveway filming, giving us space to soak it all in for a few minutes.

"Hi, Katie," Dylan said as we walked toward them. He bounced up and down. "I'm your brother."

"Me too," Jared chimed in.

With no inhibitions or restraint, they ran up and hugged their big sister. I put my hand to my mouth in wonder and in awe. It was one of the happiest and most profound moments of my life. My children—all my children—were together. My daughter was back.

"Why are you crying, Mommy?" Dylan asked.

"I'm crying because I'm so happy, honey. I'm really, really happy." He looked puzzled but went on hugging his sister.

"Let's show Katie our new house," Dylan said. "I want her to see my room."

"Me too," Jared said again.

We all walked back to Katie's car to get her luggage—when I peered in the front seat, I saw Brownie, the teddy bear that I had given Katie when she was born. It was strapped in a seatbelt in the front seat. "Oh, you have your bear with you!" I said, touched that she would bring this important symbol of our connection.

"I was packed and all ready to go and then I remembered Brownie. I just had to bring Brownie. He means a lot to me. Thanks for giving him to me."

"I'm so glad that you liked him so much. I wanted you to have something to remind you of me and remind you that I loved you."

Dylan and Jared gathered at Katie's sides and grabbed at Brownie. "Let me see," they said.

"Chrisy gave me this when I was born, and I've snuggled with him every night since then. He's my favorite bear."

"Cool," Dylan said. He and his brother took their sister's hands and led her into the house. "We have a bunch of teddy bears too. Come and see."

They pointed out each room on the main floor and then led her to the guest bedroom next to mine and Joe's. We'd already dubbed it "Katie's room"; it was bright yellow, the queen bed adorned with yellow and blue. It looked like a girl's room; it was *our* girl's room.

I followed behind my three children, watching quietly as Dylan and Jared showed off their bedrooms and favorite toys, their bathroom and toothbrushes. It was surreal to watch them so easily and beautifully come together as siblings.

What an amazing sister and daughter Katie was, to drive six hours on her own to meet her birth mother and family. She was brave. She was strong. Maybe she had gotten that from me. She was interacting so well with the boys and me, but there were moments when she was quiet and I worried she was overwhelmed. Then again, it was a lot to take in.

The next part of the carefully planned day came quickly. Becky, her family, and my mom and dad arrived at the designated time to meet their niece and granddaughter. Becky didn't hesitate to grab and hold her niece again. "I remember so vividly taking you from Chrisy's arms and walking you down the hallway to give you to Dennis and Cindy. It seems like it was just yesterday. I just knew I'd hold you again someday."

My mom also held tight to her granddaughter. "I held you when you were just hours old, and again when you were about a year old." My mom and Becky had made a visit to Katie and her parents when Becky was in Utah. They'd only told me about it after the fact, but I was fine with it. It was as though they'd done a little spying for me; a check-in to make sure she was doing okay.

"Hi, sweetheart," my dad said as he hugged Katie, pecked her on the cheek, and clasped her hand, tears brimming in his eyes. "It's good to finally meet you." Several times throughout the day, he shook his head in awe and said: "You and your grandma sure do look alike. You really do."

They did. Looking at my mom and Katie standing side by side, there was no question she was one of us. She was part of our family. I watched with pride as she interacted with her brothers, her grandparents, her aunt and uncle, and her nieces and nephew throughout the day. She was so incredibly mature, exuding such grace as she answered our many questions, told us stories about her life and her family, and asked her own questions in turn.

As I watched her, though, I knew that her outward calm was likely matched by inward anxiety. *How could you not be anxious, meeting your birth mother and family for the first time at eighteen?* When she looked at us, I imagined that she was wondering what life would have been like if she had grown up here. I wondered too.

After dinner, we gathered around Katie as she opened gifts from Becky and Grandma and then from me. She paused to read the framed picture and poem that I gave her:

She wasn't where she had been.
She wasn't where she was going . . . but she was on her way.
And on her way she enjoyed
Food that wasn't fast,
Friendships that held,
Hearts glowing,
Hearts breaking,
Smiles that caught tears,
Paths trudged and alleys skipped.
And on her way she no
longer looked for the answers
but held close the two things she knew for sure:
One, if a day carried
strength in the morning,
peace in the evening,
and a little joy in between,
it was a good one . . .
and two, you can live
completely without
completely understanding.

Tears streamed down her cheeks and mine. "Thank you, Chrisy," she said as she got up and hugged me.

"I thought it was perfect for you." When I saw the framed poem in the store, I knew instantly I needed it for Katie. I truly hoped and believed that she lived completely, even without a total understanding of why I'd given her to Dennis and Cindy so many years ago.

Then it was my turn to open my gift from Katie. I unwrapped the package and saw the purple wooden picture frame that she had made and painted. The words *Chrisy and Katie, Reunited* were painted on it.

Its beauty made up for all the homemade cards and pictures and art projects that I'd missed over all of these years—the handmade tokens she would have brought home from preschool and kindergarten and grade school. There was surely a handprint of hers in a clay cast somewhere; handmade gifts and cards for Mother's Day, Thanksgiving, and Christmas. Cindy had all of those, as she should. I was receiving the same type of handmade gifts from Dylan and Jared, and now I had this beautiful handmade and heartmade frame from Katie to add to the collection.

Later that night I got to tuck Katie in bed for the first time. "Do you want a backrub?" I asked tentatively, not wanting to overstep her comfort zone. "I give your brothers backrubs every night before bed, just like Grandma Donna used to give me."

She nodded. "I love backrubs."

I sat next to her on the edge of the bed and gently rubbed her back, thinking what it must have been like for her adopted mother to rub her back as a little girl. It was strange to be looking at this lovely young lady, who was part of me, who had grown inside me, whom I'd given birth to. We had the same hair, lips, dimples, and smile. She also told me we had the same ears. I'd never thought about our ears.

We spoke a few words here and there about how good this all was, but then we were both quiet; no words were needed. It was just a few minutes, because I didn't want to make her uncomfortable. I just wanted her to feel loved.

I leaned over, gave her a kiss, and got up to turn out the lights. "Good night, sweetheart. I love you, and I'm so happy you are here."

"I love you too, Mom. Good night."

CHAPTER 49

August 17, 2003

"Can I ask you something, Mom?"

"Yes, you can ask me anything you want," I answered, bracing myself for what was coming as we drove down the interstate highway toward downtown Minneapolis. We were having a girls' day, a mother-daughter day, in our busy first weekend together.

"Did you think about keeping me?"

"Oh, of course I did, Katie. Off and on, I would think about it. And it was a very difficult decision. But bottom line, I just didn't think I would be a very good mom, honey. I was still trying to figure out who I was, trying to make my way in the world, and I just knew I couldn't give you the stability you needed."

What I did not tell her, of course, was that I considered killing myself because I was so distraught about becoming pregnant with her. Because I felt like a selfish loser, and I didn't want to disappoint my parents or interrupt my plans for school and my career. I also did not tell her how close I came to terminating the pregnancy. I loved her so much. That's what she needed to know and understand. I would do anything for her, and I didn't want to make her hurt any more than she already may have over the years.

"What about my dad? What did he think about all of it?"

"Your dad, whose name is Jim, was supportive of my decision. He was really good through it all." A vision of Jim asking me to marry him flashed before me. I would tell her that another time.

"Do you have pictures of him that I can see?"

"Yes, I do, of course. I only have a few and you can have them if you want. We'll get them out when we get back home, okay?" I felt bad then that I hadn't thought to send pictures of her dad to her over the years, but Jim was so far removed from my life that I rarely thought about him. I reached over to her in the passenger seat and squeezed her hand. She squeezed back, and we continued down the highway with her hand in mine.

"If you want to meet him, I'm sure he'd be okay with that," I offered, even though I hadn't talked to him in about sixteen years.

"Maybe someday I will, but not right now," Katie said, her gaze turning out the window. She paused for a minute. Then it came: "I have another question."

"Sure, anything. You can ask me anything you want."

"Did you consider having an abortion?"

Oh shit. I thought I had dodged that bullet for now. I figured that she would ask me that someday, but not this soon.

"I did, Katie. I thought about it because, as I said, I was not ready to be a mom. And I'm so so glad that I didn't do that and that I had you and that you are here. I love you so much and I'm so proud of you. I just can't express enough how proud I am of you."

She was quiet for a minute while she let it sink in. *God, don't let her ask me any more details. I don't want her to know how close I came to terminating the pregnancy. And God, please help her not hate me for what I already said.*

"I'm glad you had me too," Katie said. "I really love you, Mom."

A weight lifted off my shoulders. "I hope you're not mad at me for telling you that. But I want to be honest with you. You have a right to know all of this."

"I'm not mad," Katie said, both of her hands now holding onto my free hand in her lap.

"Good. I was worried about that. Again, I want to be honest. I also want you to know that I don't look down on anyone who makes that decision. It's a personal decision, and I think it's important that women have a right to choose. I'm just really glad I chose you."

"Me, too," she said.

While we both grew quiet, I continued to talk to her in my head. *Oh yes, me too, my dear. You will never know how glad I am that I had you and how grateful I am that you came back to me. I am blessed beyond measure that I found the very best parents for you and that you love and accept me. I am the luckiest lady in the world*

From: Katie Schultz
To: Chris Bauer
Sent: Tuesday, August 19, 2003, 11:21 PM
Subject: Thanks for everything

Chrisy,
I just want to begin by saying thank you. Thank you so much for everything. For your bravery in giving me up for adoption, for the unconditional love you've given me for the last eighteen years, and for the open arms with which you received me this past weekend. I cannot tell you how truly wonderful this weekend was and how much it meant to me. I loved our walk around the lake, our morning snuggling in my bed, our talks, and just being with you.

I also loved watching you with Dylan and Jared. You are such a patient, understanding, and absolutely wonderful mother. I'm so proud of you. You are such a strong and loving person. I am in awe of you and all the wonderful things you are doing in life.

As I was showing your picture to my family and friends they couldn't stop making remarks as to how beautiful you are. You are one gorgeous mother, inside and out. I'm so glad I have your eyes, your dimples, your cute ears, and your spunk.

Meeting you has filled in the missing piece of my heart and made my life feel so complete. Thank you again, Mom . . .

The thoughts of our wonderful weekend helped me survive the atrocious day I had. I ended up babysitting the devil children (you know, the kids I talked about from last summer). About an hour after I returned home on Monday, the dad called telling me about how his sitter bailed and how he desperately needed me. I felt really sorry for him and took the job. It was pretty horrible, but it paid, so that was good. Enough about me, how was your day?

Did you visit Dylan's school? If so, how was it? Did he find out his teacher and all that good stuff? I hope elementary school is as wonderful for him as it was for me. I just know he'll make tons of friends and have a great time.

Gosh, it's 11:13 p.m. And I am still awake. This is pretty incredible. I really am not a late-night person. I should get to sleep soon. Well, good night, dear mother. Send a hello to everyone there for me.

Love ya,
Katie

From: Chris Bauer
To: Katie Schultz
Thursday, August 21, 2003, 8:41 AM
RE: Thanks for Everything

Hello Beautiful Daughter,
Thank you for your sweet, thoughtful, eloquent note. I had hoped to get an email off to you sooner, but the little fellows keep me too busy. I'm so happy that you feel so good about our time together!! I too feel that a void has been filled in my life, and it's just so amazing that everything has turned out so right. I thank God for you, for your mom and dad, for my family's support, and for bringing us back together again. I admire and respect you so much—you are such a "with-it" young woman . . . everything I wasn't at your age.

I'm already looking forward to our next get-together. I went for a walk on the trails yesterday and was especially missing you. The boys are still talking about their Katie, enjoying using your toothpaste, and putting their toothbrushes next to yours.

I told Dylan I was writing you a note and asked if he wanted to tell you anything. "Just tell her I love her," he said. He is such a sweetheart—and can be a stinker. Thanks for your kind words about my parenting skills. I do have days where I think I'm doing just a great job and others when I think I'm lousy. I think that just goes with the territory.

Dylan did have his orientation yesterday—it was geared more toward parents, just thirty-five minutes of someone talking while we sat in chairs. I came prepared with paper and crayons for Dylan and Jared. But Dylan used his to write a sign that said "Boo, you stink." Lovely. (He certainly shares our spunk!) We need you as our positive role model. The kids will greatly benefit from having such a wonderful sister!

I love you, Katie! You are also beautiful inside and out—just radiant!

Now I'd best get going. The boys are out in the garage playing—waiting until we go to the pool, where we are meeting some friends today. Jared is in his undies though, so I better get him dressed. Good luck with the devil children.

We LOVE you!
Chrisy and all the boys

CHAPTER 50

Winter 2004

Being a stay-at-home mom doesn't mean that you don't have goals—they're just very different goals. For example, rather than increasing revenue on XYZ account by 20 percent, my goals were more like making it through the day without a fight between the kids or actually getting Jared to get in the pool at swimming lessons.

On this particular winter morning, when Joe was traveling for work, my goal was to get the driveway snowplowed before I took the boys to school. I had them up, fed, and dressed with more than half an hour to go before I had to drive Dylan to school and Jared to preschool. There was plenty of time to plow while they watched cartoons.

Dylan agreed to watch Jared, and with that I set out on my mission. I suited up in full plowing gear—snow pants, boots, jacket, hat, gloves—and to my pleasant surprise got the snowblower started on the second pull. *I am woman, hear me roar!* I thought as I cut straight lines through the snow, cold mist blowing back in my face. The fresh air was brisk and refreshing, and I felt productive and excited; it was a good way to start the day.

When the driveway was about halfway cleared, I saw Dylan peering out of the garage door from the corner of my eye. He yelled something and began waving something in his hands as he leaned out the door. I shut off the snowblower, albeit tentatively, as I had some worry I wouldn't I'd be able to get it going again.

"Hi, honey, what do you need?" I asked.

"Can we play Xbox? We wanna play Xbox," he said as he waved a game in his hands.

"No, honey, you don't have that much time. I'm just about done and then we're going to leave for school," I explained.

Disappointment washed over his mischievous little face. He'd just recently purchased the Xbox game system with money he'd received for his seventh birthday and Christmas. We held out as long as we could on letting him get it; once they get started on games, we'd heard, there's no turning back. There was something about boys and their electronic toys.

"I'll be in soon, so don't play it," I added loudly, to which he replied with a giant, "Ahh, Mom, you're so mean!"

"You can play after school," I said and turned back toward the snowblower.

The door slammed shut, and briefly, just briefly, I thought, *He may just do something naughty. No, he wouldn't do that, would he?*

I fired up the snowblower again and moved the remaining snow as fast as I could. I put the machine back in the garage and then did a quick scan of the driveway. Oh, it felt good to accomplish that before eight thirty, a good start to the day.

But as soon as my hand hit the doorknob leading from the garage into the house, things quickly changed. The handle wouldn't move. I jiggled it again. *Maybe it's just stuck. No, he didn't? He wouldn't, would he? He did. That little shit locked me out.*

I pounded on the door. "Dylan, open this door right now. I mean it, Dylan. You are in *big* trouble!" No response. I put my ear up to the door and couldn't hear a thing.

Maybe, just maybe the front door was open from when I let the dog out. I walked around to the front and tried it. Locked. I pounded again and rang the doorbell several times. But I knew exactly where they were. I trudged through the snow around the side and then the back of the house, down the sloping backyard and around to the windows of our walkout basement. As I suspected, I could see a light shining through the crack under the door to the playroom. They were shut in the playroom—with no windows or phone and tucked deep in the back of the house—playing Xbox.

"God damn it, Dylan!" I shouted, pounding on the window. "You are in trouble! Big trouble." I was livid. In one click of a lock, my day had completely changed.

I trudged back uphill and over to my neighbor's house. "Can I use your phone? I'm locked out of the house." She obliged and then couldn't help but laugh as I told her the story of why I was locked out.

I dialed our phone number, and it rang and rang and rang. After my anger began to subside, I started getting worried that my four- and seven-year-old boys were locked alone in the house.

My next move was to call the Maple Grove police department. The officer arrived about twenty minutes after I called, and he, like my neighbor, chuckled when I told him exactly how I'd been locked out. He also understood my concern, but he couldn't get into my house without breaking windows.

"Ma'am, I think your best bet is to call a locksmith."

You've got to be kidding me.

By the time the locksmith arrived, hours had passed, and I vacillated between being extremely pissed off and laughing about it myself. I had this to add to a few other good stories about my oldest son.

"Stay right there; I'll be back up to pay you in a minute," I told the locksmith as soon as I stepped over the threshold. I marched down the basement stairway and into the playroom, where I threw open the door and caught them in the act. Dylan, game controller in his hand, jumped in surprise, his eyes growing wide.

Jared, a simple observer, was sitting quietly next to him, hands in his lap, his eyes as big as saucers.

"You are in huge trouble, mister. You locked me out!" I screamed.

"I didn't mean to lock you out, Mom. Really," he denied.

"Dylan Bauer Schmelz, I've been locked out for two hours and worried sick about you two."

"It hasn't been that long; it's only been a few minutes," he announced emphatically, while Jared sat next to him, hands in his lap, clueless about the severity of what his older, always naughtier brother had really done.

"Get going now," I demanded, leading them back upstairs to pay the locksmith and get Dylan to school—well over two hours late.

Dylan's consequence for this infraction was to pay me back for the $70 locksmith bill and lose the Xbox for a month. This was just one of my many adventures as a mother. You just never knew what a day with kids could bring. And all before noon.

CHAPTER 51

Spring 2004
Life is what happens to you when you are making other plans. John Lennon's words rang especially true for me in the spring of 2004. Life sideswiped me again and caused a great big crash.

"Are you having an affair?" I asked Joe again, looking him straight in the eyes. He was lying on the floor. I was sitting on the couch. He looked up at me and locked his big brown puppy eyes with mine.

"No," he replied, calmly and clearly. He didn't flinch.

Still, I didn't believe him. I asked again. "Do you swear on the Bible and on your father's grave that you are not having an affair?"

"Yes," he said again, just as calmly.

I wanted to believe him; I really did. "But something is wrong," I pleaded. "You're distant and moody and weird. And, most of all, you're being an asshole. I'm getting tired of it, Joe. Really tired of being treated like shit."

He was moody and irritable and distant, so distant—both emotionally and physically. I had to walk on pins and needles around him. He went ballistic about anything and everything. He was not himself. He got angry at the strangest things. He became obsessed with the fact that I wore Birkenstock sandals. "Those are hideous. Why do you wear those?" I wore them because they were comfy and easy to take on and off when I was busy chasing kids and a dog.

He hated what I cooked for dinner, even if it was something I made before that he'd never commented on. He got mad if he came home and there were dishes in the sink. He hated that I volunteered us to be Cub Scout leaders for Dylan. He hated the fact that I had kept my name. Yes, twelve years after the fact, he brought that up. Joe hated everything about me, most everything he once loved.

"I just don't know if I want to be married anymore. I don't know if this is what I want."

"You've got two beautiful, healthy kids and a good wife. I know I'm far from perfect, but I'm willing to work on things. I'm willing to go to counseling, but you don't want to. You've also got a great career, a beautiful house. What more do you want? What do you want from me?"

"I don't know if I want this marriage. I just don't know if I want to be married to you anymore. It shouldn't be this hard. It shouldn't be this much work."

He'd told me this a few months ago too, that he didn't know if he wanted to be married anymore. I should have known then. Deep down, I think I did know, but what could I do if he wouldn't tell me the truth?

"Well you better figure it out, Joe. I'm getting tired of you not being here and not wanting to be here when you do show up. I feel like I'm raising Dylan and Jared on my own. The boys and I deserve better."

While I was on top of the world from having Katie back in my life and mothering two healthy boys who were now in first grade and preschool, I was at rock bottom in my marriage, and I didn't know how to fix it. "Let's try counseling again. We only went a few times and that's not going to fix anything. It's going to take work."

"Counseling doesn't do any good," he said. "They're just trying to make money off us."

With those ignorant words, I got up and left the room, plodding up the steps to Jared's room. I stepped into the room and found him lying with his head toward the bottom of the bed. I smiled. He was a flipper in bed, tossing and turning, flipping and flopping.

Gently, I picked him up and turned him around so his head was at the top of the bed and on the pillow. I lay down next to him to watch him and admire his beauty, his innocence. His lips were slightly parted and I could hear his gentle, rhythmic breathing. It was the kind of sleep that comes when you don't have a care in the world, when your job in life is simply to learn, laugh, and grow. Just how it's supposed to be when you're a kid.

His slow, steady breath helped calm me; I needed to be calmed. I felt stressed and tired, mentally and physically. I felt so alone. Even though I had a husband, two boys, and a dog in the house with me, I felt so incredibly and frightfully alone and exhausted.

Joe had been incredibly busy with work, in the past few months alone traveling to Miami, Chicago, Dallas, New York, San Diego, and Vancouver. I was taking care of the boys, the house, and the dog and working to get my business off the ground. It had been a busy year.

Joe's foray into corporate meeting and event production, in addition to his video work, was taking him around the world. It was exciting, especially after years of working so hard to get his business going. I was so happy for him. He'd landed some A-list clients, his revenue had quadrupled, his corporate films now involved celebrities, and his other projects involved big-name musical acts. But as his business grew big, the two of us grew apart.

On one hand, Joe was over-the-top happy and confident about his business; on the other, he was crabby and disinterested in family life. I sensed his discontent for a while and tried to figure out what was wrong. And after years of trying to get Joe to go, we finally tried counseling. We went a few times but were not thrilled with the therapist, so we gave up. We had struggled with communicating over the years, but now it was more than that. Like a switch, Joe's personality had flipped. Something was terribly wrong.

In just a few weeks, Joe would be heading to Miami again to produce a corporate meeting. When that meeting was over, the boys and I were planning to meet him in Orlando for a much-anticipated and much-needed family vacation. Dylan and Jared were over the moon about going to Disney World and Universal Studios. They could hardly wait. I too had been looking forward to it—maybe, just maybe, it would help us reconnect. I was also looking forward to getting out of the house and out of town. Maybe Joe would decide this—me, his kids, his family—was what he wanted. On the other hand, I was dreading the time together. The tension between us had become thick and meaty. You could cut it with a knife.

The phone didn't ring once the whole week he was gone. No one is too busy to make one phone call, at least not to their children. It was just plain weird, especially since Joe used to call me all the time—too much, sometimes—and now nothing. His behavior was increasingly bizarre, and it was keeping me up at night.

Two days before the boys and I were scheduled to leave for Florida to join Joe, I was tossing and turning in bed, his behavior gnawing at me. I figured I might as well make good use of my sleeplessness and start packing for the trip.

In my pajamas and slippers, I tiptoed down two flights of stairs to the basement closet where we kept our suitcases and toted them back up to the main level. I sat them down at the top of the stairs and looked toward the door leading to the garage. Something told me to go and look in Joe's car. My suspicions had risen with each day that went by and he didn't call. Something was very wrong.

I flipped the light on and stepped out into the cool air of the garage. I walked around to the driver's side of his black Lincoln Continental, opened the door, and slid onto the soft leather of the driver's seat. I did a quick scan of the car. There were papers and coffee cups scattered about, which was not unusual. I shuffled through some of the papers, but nothing was incriminating. With my left hand, I reached down and hit the button to pop the trunk, and made my way back to the rear of the car.

The trunk door opened slowly to reveal several cluttered objects—golf clubs, a gym bag, more papers. I began sorting through them, and within seconds a Bath and Body Works receipt practically jumped up at me. Gingerly, I picked up the receipt, my hand trembling with such force that it was hard to read the shaking paper. But it was there, in plain view—an itemized listing of cucumber-scented soaps, lotions, and body scrubs that I had never received.

My heart raced as I held the receipt in one hand, continuing to shuffle through the mess of items in his trunk with the other.

Nothing else stood out. But what I held in my hand was enough. It was the smoking gun. It was all I needed to get me looking for more ammunition.

With a pit in my stomach, I went back into the den and pushed the start button on my computer. It glowed in the darkness and stillness of the quiet room, projecting an aura of eerie foreboding as I set my fingers on the keyboard and began to search.

I went to the Sprint website and entered his cell phone number. It asked me for a password, and after trying a few numbers, his account information was right in front of my face. In a few more clicks of the keyboard, the mysteries of the last year had been solved to reveal the very ugly truth.

Line by line and page by page, the invoices listed hundreds and hundreds of phone calls to numbers in Vancouver, British Columbia, some just minutes apart. They went on day after day after day. Month after month, these crazy, obsessive calls—8:01 a.m., 8:03 a.m., 8:04 a.m., 8:10 a.m., 9:00 a.m.—on and on and on. Hundreds, perhaps thousands of them. And they had all begun around the time Joe became a different man.

In that one instant, it felt like my heart stopped and my lungs didn't work. I couldn't remember how to breathe.

It was like a hard punch in the stomach. Not only was I devastated at Joe's betrayal, he had lied to me over and over again. That was almost worse. Joe had looked me straight in the eyes and lied, for *months*.

As I sat there trying to remember how to breathe, I felt a range of emotions that I didn't know I was capable of all at one time: Intense sadness. Anger. Fear. Worry. Rage. It was the first time I had experienced true rage, and it was an awful feeling.

A lump rose in my throat. I reached my shaking hand up to touch the letters and lines on the glowing computer screen. I looked up dates when he'd been particularly edgy or mentally absent. Days when I'd ask, "What is wrong with you?" Like during Jared's fourth birthday party, when we were playing games outside and he kept sneaking downstairs to "work." I kept calling him to join us. "Come on, it's your son's party. Work can wait."

Then it was my birthday, when the gift and card from him came with no sentiment at all. He was simply going through the motions between calls to his girlfriend. And Christmas, where a family picture of us in front of the fireplace shows Joe with a look that clearly says his mind was miles away. Now, I knew his mind had actually been a couple thousand miles away, with some woman in Canada.

That son of a bitch. That fucking asshole. He lied to me for so long, so many times. He was living another life, a double life. While I was home caring for family and our home, he was traveling the world and fucking some other woman.

I needed to find out who "the other woman" was. I needed to find out more about who was behind these numbers. Like a fighter getting ready for battle, I felt the adrenaline pumping through my veins with acute intensity.

My hand shook and my heart pounded as I picked up the phone and dialed one of the numbers listed on the invoice. I hit the end button just as quickly and put the phone back down. No, I couldn't do it. Instead, I went back to the garage to dig out my secret stash of cigarettes, hidden in a wicker basket on top of the stand-up freezer. It was my occasional indulgence, but never in front of the kids.

My trembling hands made it hard to light the match; it took me a few strikes to get it going and then to light the cigarette. I took a few deep drags and walked back into the house, watching the cigarette glowing in the dark along with my computer screen. I'd never smoked in our house before, but I didn't care now.

I picked up the phone again and started calling the numbers. On one number a woman's voice. I hung up, dialed the other number—another female voice. I hung up.

Panic. Anger. Fear. They rushed over me like a tidal wave. My breathing was quick and shallow.

Fuck. I knew it. I knew it. I knew it. That fucker lied to me. God damn that son of a bitch. He could have at least had the dignity to tell me the truth.

I called the numbers again. I dialed right. Yes, it was "the other woman." I hung up. Were there more than one?

Then my phone rang; the caller ID showed it was the number I'd just dialed. I let it ring. Ring. Ring. On the fourth, I steeled myself and picked it up.

"Hello."

"Who is this and why do you keep calling my cell phone and home phone and hanging up?"

"This is Joe's wife, and I want to know why the fuck you are talking to my husband all the time?"

A slight pause before she said: "We're good friends."

"Yeah, right. You're friends. He is married and has two kids, by the way. You bitch."

"No, we're just friends. You can ask him."

"How fucking stupid do you think I am?"

I hung up. I was devastated and demoralized. How could he do this to me? How? We had been partners, lovers, friends, and confidants for twelve years. Yes, we'd had our ups and downs like any couple—maybe more than other couples—but I'd never thought he was capable of this. Never. Why didn't he just leave first? Why didn't he file for divorce and then have a girlfriend?

I wanted to run and scream and cry and hit him. But I couldn't do any of those things. I had two little boys sleeping upstairs. Instead I grabbed a beer and sat in the dark and smoked—for hours, one after another after another—and drank beer after beer while I printed out dozens of pages of evidence.

I needed the beer and cigarettes to numb my feelings and stop the crazy thoughts that were going through my head. Thoughts like: *I should take all his clothes and possessions, put them in a pile in the driveway, and burn them. I should call all his family members and tell them that their precious little Joe is an adulterer. Or I should write and send an email to all his friends and clients and let them know what a "great guy" Joe is.*

But I didn't do those things. I didn't call Joe either. I couldn't bring myself to even hear his voice. I eventually made my way to my bed, although I didn't sleep one minute that night. Instead, I lay in bed staring into the darkness of the room, wondering what I was going to do, worried about my boys and how this would affect them.

Where would we live, where would I work after being out on my own for a few years? How devastated the boys would be to have their daddy gone.

I had not felt this level of stress and uncertainty since I was pregnant with Katie, when my world got turned upside down. Just like tonight, there were nights when I didn't sleep at all—when every fiber, nerve, and muscle in my body was on high alert, when I could feel my heart pounding rapidly in my chest and I struggled to get enough air to breathe, when I didn't know how I would survive.

When morning finally came, I did my best to put on a happy face for Dylan and Jared. They didn't seem to notice my puffy, red eyes or the smell of cigarettes on my clothes and in my hair. They only had one thing on their mind: Disney World.

"How many more sleeps, Mom, until we go to Disney World? How many more?"

"Just two more sleeps, guys."

"Yeah! Just two sleeps and we're going to Disney World!" Dylan shouted. "And we get to see Daddy. Yeah! I miss Daddy! I love Daddy!"

Jared joined in, jumping up and down and cheering. They were so excited about this long-talked-about vacation, but pure dread washed over me. How could I go and face him? How could I face this man who had completely betrayed me? If I saw him now, I would want to run up to him and kick him and pound my fists on him and yell to our boys, "Your daddy just wrecked us, wrecked our family."

I wanted to cancel the vacation so badly. The thought of going to Florida made me sick. How could I face him? How could I go and pretend like I was having a good time?

I would cancel. Yes, I had to cancel.

But one look back at the boys' excited faces and I knew I couldn't disappoint them. What kind of mom would do that? They would remember forever that Mommy had canceled the Disney trip. In their eyes and memories, it would be my fault.

I dropped Dylan off at elementary school and took Jared to preschool. Soon after that, my cell phone started ringing. I didn't answer the first five times he called.

The sixth time, I did.

"How could you, Joe. How could you do that to me? You've been lying and living a double life. You're a liar and a cheater!" My anger morphed into grief; I began sobbing.

"She's just a friend, Chrisy, a really good friend. That is all it is."

"How fucking stupid do you think I am, Joe? Jesus Christ. Give me a break."

"She's a friend who has been helping me work through some things," Joe said.

"Well maybe she should meet you in Florida instead of me. Because I don't think I'm coming."

"You can't do that to the boys. You can't cancel. That's selfish."

"Don't talk to me about selfish, you asshole. Maybe you should have thought about all the consequences of your actions before you had an affair. So, is she a good fuck?!"

"Calm down."

"Don't tell me to calm down. You don't just calm down when you find out your husband is having an affair." I hung up.

As soon as I could breathe again, I called my mom. I needed to tell her what was going on and ask her what she thought I should do about going to Florida. Being the great mom she always was, she just listened and said she supported whatever I decided.

God, I wanted so badly to cancel the trip, to stay home and grieve. But in the end, I didn't. I couldn't do that to Dylan and Jared. It would have crushed them not to go. So I did what any good mom would do. A few days after finding out my husband was cheating on me, I took my two boys to Florida and was greeted by him at the airport.

The boys ran to Joe with unbridled enthusiasm and jumped into his arms. I just looked him in the eyes and didn't say a word. It would be a very long five days.

As I watched thousands of other families having fun and laughing in Disney World over the next few days, I was crying. I cried while we were on the rides. I cried when we were off the rides. I cried while we were waiting in line. I cried at a restaurant when the Crosby, Stills & Nash song "Our House" played over the sound system.

Our house, is a very, very, very fine house.
With two cats in the yard . . .
Life used to be so hard but everything is easy cuz of you and our
la la la la la

Joe and I talked about the situation off and on when we could steal a few minutes away from the kids. He continued to deny the affair even though he was caught red-handed. His story was that he'd been so irritable and crabby because he couldn't decide if he should stay with me or go into a relationship with Megan, but they were just friends for now.

He told me that the main problem was that I just wasn't "into him enough." He told me "the name thing" still bothered him; yes, twelve years after he married me and said he supported my desire and right to keep my name. He also told me: "I want someone who worships me."

"The only person I worship is God, and maybe I would have been more 'into you' if you would have been around more, and interested in family life, and helping around the house and with the kids," I explained. "There is only so much of me to go around."

He said he'd been struggling with the decision to stay or go, and getting caught helped him decide. From the bed just feet across from him in our hotel room, I could see that he was relieved with his decision. He was sleeping as if he hadn't a care in the world. I, on the other hand, couldn't sleep at all and experienced for the first time in my life the desire to physically hurt someone.

Growing up, I was incredulous when I learned that people are more likely to be hurt or killed by someone they know than a stranger. I just couldn't grasp it. While my family was not perfect, we would certainly never inflict physical harm on one other. No way. We loved each other. We stood by each other. We were family.

But now, I understood. Of course, I would never act on it, but I understood. It would have been so easy for me to get up from my bed and go smack his smug face again and again and again. Instead, I turned over and looked at my peacefully sleeping son lying next to me.

One of the days in Orlando, I stayed in bed and let Joe take the boys for the entire day. I made it through the vacation, even though the boys kept asking me in Florida and when we got home: "Why are you crying, Mommy?"

What I wanted to say, of course, what formed in my mind and on my lips so many times, was: "I'm crying because Daddy cheated on Mommy. Daddy has a girlfriend."

But I didn't say it. I couldn't do that to these precious, innocent little people. They loved their daddy so much, and I didn't want them to hurt any more than they would when they learned of our relationship's demise.

CHAPTER 52

Early in our marriage, I told Joe that if he ever cheated on me, I'd divorce him. Always true to my word, I did.

A few weeks after our return from Florida, Joe asked if we could reconcile. But there was no emotion in it. It was a very casual question, similar to how he'd ask if I wanted to go out for dinner. If I said yes, he said, everything would be all right.

I said no. I said no because the lies continued even after he got caught and a heartfelt apology never came.

"Boys, your daddy and I have something important to tell you," I said as we gathered the family together in the living room. Dylan sat on Joe's lap and I put Jared on mine.

"Are we going to Florida again?" Jared asked, still smitten with the trip we had taken weeks earlier.

"No, we're not going to Florida," I said. "But that sure was fun, wasn't it?"

"Our news is that Mom and I are going to live in separate houses," Joe said, just as we had planned. "Sometimes moms and dads decide they can't live together anymore and so they get separate places to live, but we'll still see each other."

I bit my tongue as he explained the situation to them. I wanted to add: "Dad met his so-called soul mate in a bar when he was on a business trip to Vancouver and would rather be with her than with us." But, of course, I didn't. I'd taken the high road all along on this journey, and I couldn't veer off course now. I was better than that.

"So, you're getting divorced?" Dylan asked. "There's a few kids in my class whose parents are divorced."

"Yes, we're getting divorced," I admitted. "But we'll still be a family. It's just a different family. We won't live together, but we'll still get together for your birthdays and holidays and stuff."

I hated saying that—even if it didn't sound so bad, it would suck. It would suck for the kids. It would suck for me. They would hate going back and forth between houses. I would hate for them to leave me every other weekend. I wanted to be with them all the time. I didn't want to miss out on their experiences.

"Cool," Dylan said. "That means I'll get two bedrooms and two bikes and more toys, right?"

Joe and I looked at each other quizzically. It wasn't the reaction we had expected.

"Yep," said Joe. "That will be cool, huh?"

"Yay, more toys," Jared said, but I could tell his little brain was trying to grasp what this really meant.

"Well, you'll get some new things," I explained, "but the important thing to remember is that even if we don't live together, we still love our family, and Dad and I love you so much. That will never change."

Joe found a townhouse to rent a few miles away, and the only things he took from our house were his clothes and personal belongings. He left everything else to me. He left the material things like the furniture, the dishes, and décor, as well as the emotional things, like little boys who cried because they were sad and didn't understand, little boys who were angry that their lives had been turned upside down.

CHAPTER 53

With the speed of a mother in fight-or-flight mode, I bolted up the stairs that led from the living room to the bedrooms. I was following the sounds of pounding, thumping, and crashing, and as soon as I reached the top of the stairs, I could also hear crying. The sounds were all coming from Dylan's room.

I pushed opened the door to find Dylan in the middle of his bedroom in the midst of chaos, wild with anger. He was throwing books and toys and balls and Legos, anything that he could get his hands on. His eyes were red, his cheeks were wet with tears, and his teeth were clenched in frustration.

He was in pain—pain from deep down, from the heart, from the gut. My heart broke.

"Sweetie, calm down," I said as I rushed to him and wrapped my arms around his arms and bony little waist. He flailed and screamed; I flinched as I worked to avoid getting hit.

"Dylan, stop, honey. What's wrong?" I asked, even though I knew the answer before he said it.

"Why doesn't Daddy love us anymore? Why did he leave us?" His neck veins bulged and his face turned an even deeper shade of red. "I hate Daddy, and I hate you too."

"Ohhh sweetie, Daddy still loves you. He loves you and Jared so much, and so do I." Jared was asleep in his room across the hall, and I prayed he wouldn't wake up from the commotion; he didn't need to see or hear this.

"Then why did he leave? Why doesn't he want to be here with us anymore?"

I struggled to tame the thrashing arms of a seven-year-old who was pumped up on adrenaline and to explain what was hard for me, at age thirty-eight, to understand. How can you just quit one life so you can have another?

It would be so easy to tell Dylan what really happened; what really broke us up. I so wanted to say to him, "Well, Daddy is dating a woman who is twenty-eight and lives in Canada. He wants her to move here and he told me that I'd really like her. So, you see, I had to divorce him."

But, of course, I can't say those things—I am the mom, and I have to be mature and responsible and levelheaded. "Well, sometimes, mommies and daddies decide that maybe they didn't marry the right person or they can't get along anymore, so they go their separate ways. But that doesn't mean we're not a family; it's just that we're a different family than before."

He broke free from my grip and started ripping the comforter off the bed and pulling at the sheets. I grabbed a pillow and put it on the bed and punched it.

"Hit this. Hit the pillow. Hit it hard, because it's okay to be mad. Take your frustrations out on the pillow."

His eyes darted to the pillow and he began punching it with all his might. I watched him as he hit and hit and hit until he didn't have any more in him, until he collapsed in my arms. I held him tightly but gently, the tension slowly releasing from his body. I knew then just what he and I needed.

I picked him up and cradled him in my arms like a baby, like I used to and often still longed to, and walked slowly to the spare bedroom—"Katie's room"—where the rocking chair sat. We'd talked about giving the rocking chair away when we moved because we didn't need it anymore. But I could just never bear to part with it. And now I knew why. I would need it again.

We settled into the chair, its blue cushion lightly stained with formula and faded from the sun, sat in the dark stillness of the room, and rocked. Back and forth, back and forth, we rocked, and as Dylan's tears dried up, mine began.

CHAPTER 54

March 2005
Having two homes, two bedrooms, and two sets of toys sounds very appealing to kids, but then reality sets in and the fun wears off.

The boys quickly tired of having to go back and forth between Joe's house and mine, and I quickly tired of packing and unpacking suitcases and the emotional baggage that came with them. I had primary custody, so Dylan and Jared lived with me and spent every other weekend or one night a week with Joe. His work continued to take him on the road a lot of the time, so we often had to adjust the schedule to accommodate his travel as well as my own. We made it work as best we could, because we had to.

I was thrilled when the time came for me to travel—for me to go see my girl—and the schedule was adjusted for me. Katie was in Germany in a semester-abroad study program, and I decided to visit her while she was on her spring break. Dennis and Cindy decided to join us a few days into the trip. This would be by far the longest that I'd been away from Dylan and Jared, as well as the longest period of time I'd ever spent with my daughter.

My heart was filled with such joy as she and I stood arm in arm in the Berlin airport, waiting for her dad and her "other mother" to arrive. To some, I'm sure Katie and I looked like siblings rather than mother and daughter. People said that to us more than a few times. "Oh, you two must be sisters!"

"Nope, I'm her mom," I'd reply proudly.

Sometimes we told our story to strangers, sometimes we didn't. Today, our story was becoming complete. Two years after Katie and I reunited, I was finally meeting Cindy and Dennis. Ironically, we had lived only three hundred miles apart over the past twenty years—in

Minneapolis and Milwaukee—yet we were meeting in Germany.

"There they are! I see my dad," Katie said.

I spotted him too, making his way through the crowd to the luggage carousel. He saw us and waved. He was exactly as I remembered from the pictures, with a big, sweet, boyish grin and kind, sparkling eyes behind his round glasses.

Next we spotted Cindy, with her big blue eyes, blonde hair, and warm smile. We watched eagerly as they retrieved their luggage—and as soon as they came through the doorway, we embraced, a big group hug.

"It's a sandwich hug," Cindy said, and I pictured her saying cute things like that to her kids growing up. She was a great mother, Dennis a great father, and it felt so good to be in their warm embrace. These were the same strong, safe arms that had rocked my daughter to sleep, the arms that had held her and hugged her through childhood triumphs and defeats. The hands that now rested on my back were the hands that had fed my daughter, bathed her, changed her, and held her fingers when she had learned to walk.

"Oh, it's so good to meet you!" I said. "Finally, to meet you after all these years—and in Germany!"

"But we know each other already," Cindy said.

She was right. We had been family for a long time. Jim, Katie's younger brother, was also along, so it was a treat to meet him too. Jim was one of the four Schultz kids—two adopted, two biological—and he was just eleven months younger than Katie, her Irish twin. Shortly after Dennis and Cindy adopted Katie, after nearly a decade of trying to have children, they got pregnant with Jim, and with Elizabeth later down the road.

I chatted with Jim as I watched Katie and her parents interact. My daughter—our daughter—was such a wonderful, beautiful person, extremely confident and kind, and I had them to thank for it. I had given Katie her life, but they had given her *a* life. I had given her those eyes, dimples, lips, and thick hair, but they had helped give her the confidence and grace to make those features so beautiful. I'd passed on my strong will and spunk, and they'd taught her how to use them constructively. Through their love and encouragement, they had conducted a beautiful symphony of nature and nurture.

We stood in the airport, one big happy family—taking pictures, hugging, crying, smiling, and laughing. Evidence again that it was all meant to be. Every part of it was meant to be.

As we left the airport, Cindy, Dennis, and I watched with pride as our Katie navigated our small group onto buses and trains and through the streets of Berlin. We let her be our guide—she'd been our guide all along.

I watched and listened as the Schultz family shared stories of vacations past, of sibling rivalries, of friends and family. They were a family that laughed often and loved much. The stories they shared added color to the picture I already had of Katie's happy childhood. As we made our way along the streets of Berlin, Cindy and I walked a few steps behind and watched Katie stroll along, holdings hands with her dad. It was touching to me that she was so comfortable and close to her dad that she would walk hand in hand with him for blocks on end.

As we followed behind them, Cindy told me stories that reinforced the divine intervention and serendipity that had brought us together twenty years ago, including a story of a moment in time that had sealed our fate.

"We'd lost touch with the Proutys, hadn't talked to them in years, until I read an article in the newspaper about Mike and Andy," Cindy explained. "And I almost didn't read that day's edition. We'd been out of town, and I had a stack of mail and newspapers to go through and was just going to throw away the papers and go to bed. But it was like something pulled me to the stack of newspapers and told me to read that day's paper. I did, and the rest is history! We got reconnected with the Proutys, who knew Becky through Andy's school, who got us to you. It was all meant to be!"

I smiled. "Yes. It was *so* meant to be. It's all part of the grand plan." The single act of her reading a newspaper article changed all our lives forever.

We walked a bit longer, and then the time was right.

"So I have to ask you about something I've wondered about for a long time. First, though, I'll say that I love the name Katie. And our Katie is a Katie; the name fits her! But I'm curious why you changed it from Elizabeth? I named her Elizabeth because that was my confirmation name."

Cindy stopped in her tracks, and I stopped alongside her. She grabbed my hand.

"Oh my gosh," Cindy exclaimed. "We loved the name Elizabeth, but we thought that was the name the nurses gave her. We didn't know it was you! So we changed it to Katie. And then when Elizabeth came along, she got that name."

"Oh, that is crazy! I guess that didn't get communicated," I said. "But that's okay, she's a Katie. It fits her," I put my arm around Cindy and gave her a quick squeeze. "Just look at her."

I was so proud of my daughter and so happy to get to know her wonderful family. I was grateful that the Schultz family was intact, that Cindy and Dennis had a strong marriage. I knew in my heart of hearts this was a great, loving, caring family with a committed, loving couple at the helm. While this brought me tremendous joy and a sense of peace, it also made me long to have a family that was complete, with a mother and father who could share the same moments and savor the joy of family as well as support each other during life's ups and downs. I wanted that. It was the only reference point I had.

Growing up in Mitchell, none of my close friends' parents were divorced. In college, only a few of my friends had divorced parents. It just wasn't what I knew. Every once and a while, I wondered if maybe I had done the wrong thing in divorcing Joe. *Maybe we should have tried harder to fix things.* If only he had been honest with me and not lied over and over again, it might not have ended the way it did. Although this made me sad, it was a sign that it was time to move on, to be open to finding someone else with whom I could share my life and my family.

CHAPTER 55

Dating could be, should be, *would* be fun. I tried to convince myself of this, but dating is not all that it's cracked up to be when you're middle-aged and have two young kids at home.

After nearly two years of being on my own and either being by myself or with other couples when the kids weren't around (I was known as "Bonus Girl"), I figured I had to get myself out there. I had to get back in the game. Because I worked out of my house and was home with the boys all the time, the easiest way to make this happen was to go online. It was time to make the effort, especially with those Match.com ads that kept telling me: "One in five relationships start online."

I wasn't ready for a serious relationship, but I just knew I needed to get out there. My interactions with adults—especially men—were limited because I was working out of the house, doing my freelance business, and spending the majority of my time taking care of Dylan and Jared. I was a busy mother of two little boys, and I wasn't exactly a hot item on the dating scene. I wanted to date. Hell, I just wanted *a* date.

I sat down at my computer one evening to begin this online journey. I registered for Match and plugged in my vital statistics—height, weight, hair color, eye color, relationship status, education, family, hobbies, work. I also wrote a profile, which included the sentence: "I am a devoted mother of three, and my children are my number-one priority." In hindsight, that was not a good marketing tool, but it was the truth.

I uploaded a photo, though I had a hard time finding one of just me. Most of my photos were of me and the boys, or me and Joe, or me and my girlfriends—hardly any existed of just me. I entered my credit card information and, with a deep breath, pushed the return button. I was officially in the game.

Within minutes of joining Match, I had several "winks." It was weird, fun, and creepy all at the same time. I decided to search and wink too, so I entered my search criteria—male, age range thirty-five to forty-five, within a twenty-mile radius of my zip code—and hit send. Within seconds, dozens of matches appeared on my screen. "You've got to be kidding me," I said aloud.

The first match in the lineup was a very familiar face. There on my computer screen, right in front of me, was Joe's picture. Of all the men in the Twin Cities, Joe appeared as my number-one match.

I laughed at both the irony and the complete sadness of it. Even though we were divorced, I still loved him. I would always love him. He was my friend; the father of my children; my family. I sat looking at his familiar eyes and easy smile. I remembered the many laughs that had come from that face long before the past two years of anger and sadness. He and the young Canadian had broken up not long after he and I separated, and I had gathered over the past two years that he dated a lot.

I just couldn't ignore this, so I sent him a wink and a note: "Hey, they say we are a great match! Want to give it a try? Ha, ha, ha. Just kidding! Your ex, Chrisy."

Within minutes, he responded: "Hey, that's funny. How are you?"

"Fine. Just giving this online thing a try. You've probably been at it a while."

He ignored that comment and wrote: "Your profile looks great, Chrisy."

I wanted to write back: "Too bad you didn't think it was so great when we were married," but I didn't. I took the high road, just as I had throughout this difficult journey of separation, divorce, and co-parenting.

Through meditation, reflection, and prayer, I had gradually let go of my anger for what Joe had done, for the infidelity and the lies. I forgave him because I knew that if I didn't, it would hurt me, not him. I forgave him because I would do anything for my boys.

Being friends with Joe was much easier than being enemies. With both boys in baseball and football, we were going to games and practices four to five nights a week and either sitting together at games or communicating and coordinating the schedules for getting the boys where they needed to be. Sometimes after games, we'd go out for ice cream or out to dinner. We were a still a family.

It was strange, this online dating thing. Everyone said it was so great, but was it that much different from meeting some guy at a bar? Not really, it was just more systematic. I did find some appealing pictures and profiles, so I took the plunge and winked. I winked at AmazingBlueEyes, and he winked back immediately. We began corresponding, and soon we had a first date set up. We agreed to meet for lunch at a restaurant near my house and near where he worked. He was waiting in the lobby when I arrived.

AmazingBlueEyes, real name Brian, did indeed have amazing blue eyes, a nice smile, and a very nice build. I would put him in the hot category. We were seated at a table in the middle of the restaurant and immediately hit it off. It was easy to talk to him since we had a lot in common. We shared a love of the outdoors. He was a big-time snow and water skier. He was active.

He asked about my kids; I told him about Dylan, Jared, and having Katie when I was nineteen. He'd also had a child at an early age—a *very* early age. He had been just sixteen when he had his son, who was now twenty and had a child of his own. Brian was a grandpa at age thirty-six.

While we hit it off and I was enjoying our lunch, I couldn't help but think how odd it seemed to be sitting in a restaurant with another man on a date. After thirteen years of being with the same person, it was strange. I thought of Joe sitting in some five-star hotel in Vancouver with his lover. I wondered if it had made him nervous, sitting there wondering if he'd run into someone he knew. If he'd thought about me and the boys at all while he was with her.

I came back to the moment and refocused on Brian. We ended our long lunch with plans for another date.

We had another date and then another. I enjoyed his company, but our lives were just too different at this point. His schedule was completely flexible and he was available every night of the week. My schedule was completely inflexible most of the time. I was with my kids all the time except one night a week and every other weekend, and I refused to get a babysitter to go on a date when it was my night with the kids. The timing just wasn't right.

I continued for just a bit longer with Match.com and learned a few things along the way, some quicker than others. Immediately, of course, I knew to ignore winks and emails from guys with online names like Here2PleezU, HotStuff35, and YourBigDaddy. I learned that many users weren't exactly honest in their online descriptions about height, weight, or employment. I learned to ignore Joe's face regularly popping up on my screen as a match.

And I also learned after a few months of dates here and there that I needed to adhere to a few dating rules. Rule #1: Do the initial meeting—i.e. "first date"—over coffee, rather than dinner or drinks. Coffee allows for a much easier exit if it's not going well, which you

can typically judge within the first ten minutes. Rule #2: Never meet at a bar. By meeting in a restaurant or coffee shop there is no chance of altered judgment, as can be the case after a glass of wine or two.

There were some nice guys out there, but at my age, most everyone comes with a couple of kids and some baggage. I couldn't help but think every time I was out with someone: *I don't want to raise anyone else's children, and I don't want anyone else raising mine.*

CHAPTER 56

Spring 2006

It was hard to know how to be a good mom to a twenty-one-year-old woman who had been raised by someone else, but I was trying.

And being a good parent means you're bound to make mistakes and have disagreements with your children. Katie and I had our first mother-daughter disagreement about three years after we were reunited.

She was staying with me for one of our girls' weekends together; Dylan and Jared were spending the weekend with Joe. "Maybe you can just live in New Zealand for a year or so before you get married," I said to Katie as we sat next to each other, propped up on our bar stools at the kitchen island, browsing through bridal magazines. "Then you can really get a feel for what it will be like, honey. It won't be the same as when you go there on vacation. You are kind of in la-la land right now."

Those words hit her like a branding iron. With hurt and anger in her eyes, she put down the issue of *Modern Bride* she held in her hands and looked at me piercingly.

I felt like an ass. Right after the words passed my lips, I knew I'd said the wrong thing, or at least said it in the wrong way. I was trying to offer some motherly advice on what it would be like to be a newlywed and live eight thousand miles away from home and family. She had only experienced being that far apart from home while vacationing for a month or two at a time. Living and working in another country so very far away would be far different than being there on vacation. And marriage could be very hard, especially those first years.

"No, we want to get married now, and it's not that easy just to live there. I knew you wouldn't be supportive. You're just anti-marriage and anti-men because of what Joe did to you."

Ouch. That stung. "No, that's not it, Katie. My relationship with Joe has nothing to do with this. I am supportive, and I really like Paul and am happy for you, but I just don't think you need to rush into getting married. Be engaged for a while. You're both so young."

They were. Katie was twenty-one and Paul was twenty. He was Katie's first boyfriend, her first real kiss, and her first love. Katie met sweet, adorable Paul the first summer after college at church camp in Wisconsin, where they were both camp counselors. They fell in love, and after a long-distance romance and visits back and forth, they got engaged on a quiet beach in New Zealand.

I adored Paul; we all did. He was cute, both inside and out, with his New Zealand accent, easygoing style, and sweet demeanor. He clearly loved Katie, but still, they were so young.

My hesitation was also tied to that fact that I was worried about my little girl—my baby whom I finally had back—going so far away. It was hard to think that she was grown up enough to be engaged, get married, and move to New Zealand.

"I'm going to go for a walk," she announced abruptly.

"Do you want me to come along?" I asked, although I knew she didn't want me, and I really didn't want to go.

"No, I want to go by myself." She grabbed her magazines from the counter, shoved them into her bag, and headed out the door.

She was pissed off. Big time. And I felt bad. I'd handled it all wrong. But I'd needed to express my concern about her going so far away and marrying so young. Deep down, my fear of her getting married and moving to New Zealand was also about the fact that I'd finally gotten Katie back in my life after all these years. Now I had to let her go again.

CHAPTER 57

September 22, 2006
Loss and letting go were things we had to learn to deal with in a short amount of time. In the span of three years, my marriage broke up and the family we had known disappeared; Katie came back into our lives and was now moving eight thousand miles away; and Joe's sister Pauline, a dear friend and a beloved aunt to the boys, lost her battle with cancer at age forty-nine. Then, a mere six weeks after Pauline's death, we buried my dad.

The call that my dad was dying came when I was at Chuck E. Cheese's celebrating Jared's seventh birthday. Joe was with me, helping me manage ten wild and happy six- and seven-year-old boys.

We had just finished eating cake and opening gifts. Wrapping paper, gift bags, and boxes littered the long, rectangular table alongside plates of half-eaten chocolate cake, cups of soda, and confetti. Balloons drifted several feet above the table, and all around us were the ringing and clanging of laughter, screams, and electronic games.

I had put my cell phone in my pocket on vibrate so I could answer it immediately if I got any calls; I was waiting for an update. When it buzzed, I grabbed it from my pocket and began walking away from the kids.

"Hold on, Mom, I can't hear you," I yelled into the phone, holding it with one hand and plugging my ear with the other. I walked quickly into the calm of the women's bathroom. "Okay, that's better now. I can hear you. How's Dad doing?"

My dad, who'd had his first heart attack nearly twenty years ago, was in the hospital and gravely ill, due mostly to an MRSA infection—an antibiotic-resistant staph infection—in his left arm, where his dialysis shunt was implanted.

"Well, not so good, honey," she conceded. "Your Dad has decided that he isn't going to do dialysis anymore."

As soon as those words registered in my brain, I crumbled. I sank to my knees, leaning my shoulders and head against the white tiled wall of the restaurant bathroom. I knew what that meant. It meant my dad was going to die. Papa, Pops, Grandpa Jim, my daddy, was going to die. This time it was for sure. His body, not just his kidneys, was worn out and would not survive without dialysis.

"He's tired," my mom added. "He's tired of fighting."

Over the years, my dad had endured numerous heart attacks, bypass surgeries, defibrillator implants, infections, and bouts of pneumonia. But he always pulled through. Even when the doctors, and the nurses, and the priests told us he wouldn't make it, he always did. Always. But he wouldn't this time. Going off dialysis was a certain death sentence.

"Okay, I'm coming home, Mom. I'm coming to the hospital. I just need to finish up here and then I'm coming. I want to be with him," I said, feeling fear and sadness and urgency and desperation.

"No, honey, come home tomorrow. It's too late, and your dad insists, absolutely insists, that you girls not drive home tonight in the dark. He said he wants you to wait until the morning."

"But I want to get there, Mom. I want to be with him when he goes."

I pictured being there at his bedside. I'd hold his weathered hand, wrinkled from age and purple and blotchy from the blood thinners and other medications he was on. And then I'd slowly, gently crawl in bed with him and lie next to him. And I'd hold him. Just like he used to hold me when I was little.

"They said it would take a couple of days; he has a couple of days left. You'll have time."

"Oh, Mom, I'm so sad," I cried into the phone. "I don't want him to go."

"Oh, honey, I know. It's hard, but we've been lucky to have him as long as we have. We really have. And he's been miserable for so long." My mom's words, always calm and steady, were soothing. "He's ready to let go."

She was right; we were lucky to have him as long as we did. But it did not make it any easier. I promised her I would leave as early as I could in the morning and that I'd see her soon.

"Tell Dad I love him! And give him tons of hugs and kisses for me. I love you, Mom."

I pushed the *end* button on my cell phone and put it back in my pocket. Then I went to the mirror to dry my eyes and collect myself. This didn't seem real. Learning that my dad was really going to die while I was standing in the bathroom at Chuck E. Cheese's on my son's seventh birthday.

I took a few minutes to gather my strength and put on a happy face as best I could. Then I walked the few steps back out into the mayhem of Chuck E. Cheese's. I told Joe what was going on. He offered to take the boys home that night and keep them as long as I needed. Then he gave me a big hug. "Tell your dad that I love him too. Please."

"I will. I promise." I recalled the memories of the two of them hanging out together. "This is going to be so hard on the boys. Dealing with all this loss in such a short amount of time," I said, thinking of Pauline.

"So, if you keep the boys here, then you'll need to bring them to Mitchell for the funeral. I'm assuming you'll want to go to the funeral too, right?"

"Absolutely, I want to be there," Joe said. "I love your dad."

Joe and my dad had been pretty close. Whenever we went home, the two of them golfed if the weather was good and ran errands together. They also loved to sneak a cigar or two out in the garage, not that you could really ever "sneak" a pungent cigar. They'd go their way and my mom and I would go ours. We also had lots of fun "double dates" over the years when my parents came to Minneapolis. We'd hit the hot new restaurants and take in a jazz show.

Lying in my bed alone, I thought of all the things that I would say to Dad in the morning, things I was so grateful I'd get the chance to tell him: that he was a great dad and that I loved him so much. That I appreciated all he ever did for me and for our family. That he'd shown me the value of hard work and tenacity.

I'd tell him I was sorry that I was such a rebellious teenager and thank him for steering me in the right direction. I'd tell him that Dylan and Jared loved him so much. That he was a great dad and grandpa. And that I was so glad and grateful that he got to meet Katie, and that she got to meet him. And that I hoped I'd been a good daughter and that I had made him proud. I was ready to tell him all of it.

I drifted in and out of sleep for a few hours until the ring of the telephone woke me up. The landline phone wasn't next to my bed, so I sprinted down the stairs and grabbed the phone in the kitchen on the fourth ring.

"Hello," I said with fear in my heart.

My mom's words echoed into the phone as soon as I answered. "Chrisy. He's gone."

The words cut me off at the knees, like a giant samurai sword swinging wildly in the dark. My whole body hit the floor, but the phone was still gripped tightly in my hand. It was the second time that news had truly knocked me all the way down to the floor; the other was a few years ago, when I'd learned that Katie wanted to meet me. Then it was the shock of happiness; now it was the shock of devastation.

"Oh, my daddy. My daddy. I wanted to be there. I wanted to be with him. I wish I would have been there. God damn it," I shouted. "I should have left right after Jared's party. Damn it!"

"Chrisy, it's okay, honey. This is how he wanted it; he wanted to be alone," she said, adding firmly, "No regrets now. We're not going to have any regrets."

She explained that he died by himself, alone in the stark, sterile, empty hospital room.

"I went out to the car to get my suitcase; I was only gone about fifteen minutes and when I came back he was gone. I thought he was sleeping at first. I couldn't believe it was that quick."

He made his exit on his own, stepping quietly from this world into the next with no one at his side, no one crying or fussing over him. I pictured him lying in bed as my mom told me more about his last minutes, and I couldn't help but wish I would have been there to say *I love you* a million times, to hug him and kiss him.

"We had a really nice talk," my mom said. "We talked about how lucky we were to have our family and how blessed our lives were with you kids and grandkids and friends and all the traveling we did. We had a good livelihood. And we talked about how we loved each other. Even through all those hard time, we always loved each other. It was one of the best talks we ever had."

I pictured my mother at his side, holding his hand, supporting him, and caring for him as she always did. "I'm so sorry, Mom. Are you okay?"

"I'm okay," she said.

"I'm coming. I'll be there as soon as I can."

In the pitch black of the September night, I drove home to South Dakota. My mind and body were on autopilot as I navigated my way out of my suburban neighborhood and onto the nearly deserted metro freeways.

Memories, soaked in years of grey matter, came floating back to the surface of my mind so fresh that they seemed real. I could feel the warmth of my dad's big, warm belly on those rare nights when I was allowed to sleep in their bed because of a storm. I could feel the cold wind dancing across my face as I held on tight to my dad from the back of a snowmobile. I could hear his voice calling out to me from the speedboat—"You're doing a good job, Chrisser"—as I tried again and again to stay upright before dropping one waterski.

As I made my way out of the metro area and into rural Minnesota, the two-lane highways became eerily dark, completely deserted. It was pitch black for much of the time. There was no moonlight nor any other lights to illuminate the roads for most of the drive. It was total darkness outside and total darkness inside my heart.

Pink Floyd's "Another Brick in the Wall" came on the radio; the rhythm and schoolchildren's chants of, "Hey, teacher! Leave those kids alone," were haunting and disorienting. I needed something to keep me alert and focused, so I pulled into the Holiday station in Windom, about 130 miles outside of Minneapolis, and bought a pack of Marlboro Lights. I hadn't smoked in a while, but I couldn't get it out of my head. I wanted my old friend nicotine to keep me awake, to soothe me.

My dad and I had both been smokers—closet smokers for a while, the two of us hiding in the garage and smoking during holidays. It was a little thing we shared. Even long after he was supposed to quit because of his heart attacks, my dad cheated and would sneak cigarettes and cigars once in a while. And he drank his red wine. He took full advantage of the oft-touted health benefits of red wine. But what the hell, he needed something; I couldn't be mad at him for that.

I smiled at that as I got back in the car and lit my cigarette. My dad and I were so much alike in many ways—headstrong, stubborn, doing things our way.

Back on the road, only the glow of my cigarette, the headlights, and the dashboard kept me from getting lost in the darkness. Between laughing and crying for the rest of the drive, I forgave myself for not driving home right after Jared's party. I forgave myself because that really must have been how he wanted to go—alone, privately, quietly, and on his own terms.

If the family had been there, it would have been harder for him to go, like it had been before. There were other times when he'd been so close to death that we'd brought in a priest to give him last rites—once at the Sioux Falls hospital and once in Rochester at St. Mary's Hospital. Circled around him and holding hands, my siblings, my mom, a priest, and I had prayed over his body, dying and motionless except for the loud, rhythmic, artificial breathing of the ventilator.

Whoosh, tap, tap, tap, whoosh. His chest rose and fell, methodically and unnaturally. Tubes came and went from his mouth and nose, arms and fingers. The lights on the heart monitors flashed numbers that were too low or too high—too *something*. The vital signs were not good; we were bracing for the end. We prayed for him and wept for him as we prepared to send him into the next world. And then we waited. And waited.

And to everyone's surprise, even the doctors', he'd decided to stay; my dad had pulled through against all odds and lived another eighteen years. In those eighteen years, he had lived to see so many things. He'd lived to see his sons buy his business, to walk his daughters down the aisle, and to welcome all of his grandchildren into the world, some sooner than others.

I thought of him and my children, all my children. Jared called him "my chocolate buddy," and Dylan loved to snuggle with him. And Katie, oh Katie—I was so glad she'd gotten to meet him and he'd gotten to meet her. Though he never said much about Katie, technically his first grandchild, I knew that it meant a lot to him to meet her. I never thought or talked much about how this impacted him, but the whole adoption journey must have been hard on him too. It was hard for my father to talk about his feelings, but there are some things you just know, without anyone saying a word.

My thoughts and memories carried me on that drive home to South Dakota, and my angel must have been helping me drive. I arrived at the hospital at five in the morning and joined Becky and my mom at his bedside.

He looked very peaceful, serene even, as I entered the room. Although it was difficult to see my dad lying there with no life in him, there was some comfort in it too. He was at peace. *He's been so unhealthy and uncomfortable for so long.* Now he looked like he was resting comfortably. With tears flowing down my cheeks, I bent down ever so gently and touched my lips to his forehead, giving him a loving kiss. Then I tenderly touched his arms and his hands, laid my head on his chest, and told him what I was going to tell him last night.

"I love you, Dad, and I'm going to miss you terribly. I'm going to miss you so much. You were a great man, a great dad, and a great grandpa. I was proud to have you as my dad. Dylan and Jared love you so much and I'm so glad you got to meet Katie. I love you, Dad.

I know you're in a better place now. Thanks for teaching me all you did. Thanks for being a great dad."

I sat next to him for a while and then hugged my mom and sister. The three of us sat with my dad's body for several hours. We talked about him and to him, though we knew his spirit wasn't in his body but around us. We cried and laughed at our memories of him.

We stayed with him for nearly three hours, until the funeral director came to get him. Then we walked through the hallways of the hospital and the loading docks to accompany his body to the hearse. The funeral director said he'd never had any family do that. We couldn't imagine doing anything but that for our beloved dad.

The three of us held hands as we stood at the dock door and watched as they rolled my dad's remains, zipped in a maroon body bag, down the ramp and into the back of the open hearse. Cries erupted from our throats as the door slammed shut and his physical body was gone from us, forever. We would never again feel his touch, hear his voice, talk to him. He was gone.

And because he was gone, they came. A steady stream of people flowed through my parent's house, sometimes slowly and gently, sometimes with more force. People expressing their sorrow; offering hugs, food, and flowers; and sharing memories.

Most of these were people I'd known my entire life. They were characters who'd helped shape our family story and held major plotlines in my dad's life. He was born near Mitchell and grew up there, so many of these people were lifelong friends—*truly* lifelong, with relationships spanning more than seventy years.

"Oh, goodness, I remember your dad delivering groceries to my house when he was not even a teenager. He could hardly see over the steering wheel!" said one woman. And there were the seventy-five-year-old men whose faces still lit up when they reminisced about playing high-school sports with my dad. "He wasn't very big, but boy, was he a tenacious player."

Then there were others I didn't know at all, but they'd been touched by my dad's kindness. "Your dad always took time to have a cup of coffee with me." "Your dad helped me out financially when I was in a pinch."

We loved hearing those stories, stories that stuck around when you lived in a small town. The blessings of small-town life were multiplied by the hundreds in times of sorrow, and I was reminded of it time and time again over those days at home.

During those days, the Bauer family came together to divide and conquer the tasks that surround a funeral. Becky was in charge of the photo collage, gathering and grouping pictures of my dad throughout his life—as a coyly smiling little boy holding a puppy; as a slightly bigger boy standing arm in arm with his little brother; as a young army man in the Korean war; as a handsome, shy-looking groom; as a father and grandfather. There were pictures of him with all his grandchildren, including one with Katie. It is the only one I have of them together.

Katie made it home for his funeral, and I was so grateful for that. She learned so much about our family and her grandfather in those few days, listening to the words of his eulogies and seeing and meeting the great number of people who attended the service and visited our home.

Joe was also there for the funeral. It seemed right to have him there. Even after all he had done and all we had been through, Joe was still part of the family and would always be. He and my dad had spent lots of time together over the years, and I just couldn't erase Joe from those memories. My loyalties had always run deep, and that wasn't changing now.

I was like my dad in that regard. He was loyal. And while he was often a man of few words (and those few words were sometimes gruff), everyone adored him. He didn't have to say much for you to know he loved you. That's just how it was. You knew he would do anything for you.

I was in charge of writing my father's obituary and the eulogy, with input from my siblings, my mom, and the grandkids. I wrote it, but I could not deliver it. I knew I couldn't speak the words that flowed freely from my fingertips to the keyboard without breaking down. So Becky, who is always good with speaking, stood up in front of friends and family and read the words that described our father and his life:

Thank you for coming today to pay tribute to Jim Bauer, a truly wonderful man. Jim was many things—he was an entrepreneur, a business leader, a community leader. More importantly, he was a good and loyal friend. He was a mentor to many and an advocate for those who needed one.

Jim was all those things, but first and foremost he was a dedicated husband, devoted father, loving grandfather, and caring uncle. He believed in the values of hard work, honesty, integrity, and fairness. Jim did not want to get ahead if it was at the expense of someone else. As successful as he was, he was equally as humble. He treated everyone he knew equally—that is, with dignity and respect—be they the janitor or the bank president. We can remember Dad telling us that you could tell a lot about a person by how they treated others.

We have many, many good memories of our dad. Weekends at the cabins, Jim was busy making beef jerky for everyone and making sure all the kids had plenty of banana popsicles. When we were little, he closed the lab for two weeks so he could take us on family vacations. Talk about a relaxing vacation . . . driving four kids to Texas in a sedan.

As busy as he was building a business and working to make Mitchell a great community, he always made time for us. He never missed one of our basketball games, gymnastic meets, or choir concerts. He was there for us, and he never stopped taking care of us. Even as adults, we couldn't leave the house without him asking: Do you have enough gas in the car? Do you need any money? Remember to watch your speed limit. It was his little way of showing us he cared.

We think it's because he cared about us and loved us so much that he willed himself to live as long as he did. Dad had his first heart attack eighteen years ago, and there were many times we didn't think he would make it. But he pulled through because he needed to be there for us. He needed to be there to walk his daughters down the aisle at their weddings; he needed to watch his sons take over the business he worked so hard to build; and he needed to see all his grandchildren come into this world . . .

We miss him terribly, but we find comfort in knowing that he lives on in all of us and that at last, he is at rest without pain, in the company of those he loved so much who have gone before him.

You fought the good fight, Dad. We love you.

CHAPTER 58

Spring 2007

My mom taught me so many valuable lessons in life simply by how she lived hers. My children did the same. They taught me great patience, true acceptance, and pure, unconditional love. They also taught me the art of forgiveness. I hadn't really been the forgiving type before. Or more accurately, I'd been a grudge holder. And that wasn't good.

I watched Dylan and Jared forgive and forget so easily and quickly with their playmates, with each other and with me, and I saw the true beauty in forgiveness. Learning to let go and to move on was the healthy thing to do. Kids know how to do it much better than adults. Kids know how to do so many things better.

Even though I would never forget what he did, I needed to forgive Joe. I had to let go or it would eat me alive. But how could I forgive someone who completely and utterly betrayed me? How could I forgive someone who looked me in the eye and lied to me? How could I forgive someone who took so long to admit his guilt and say he was sorry?

I could and I did by working at it. I read books about it. I wrote about it. I went to counseling. I talked about it with friends and family. I cried about it. I prayed about it. It took me nearly two years to release the hurt and anger, to let go of the pain that had gripped and nearly choked my heart and my head. I'm not sure what the right formula was, but finally, I was able to forgive Joe.

We'd gotten to a good place by then, to the point that we sat together at the boys' baseball games and football games. We went to school conferences together and spent most holidays together. And we talked a lot. We had to do that to be good parents. We both worked hard to keep their childhood as carefree as possible. We worked hard to have a nice family even though we were divorced. So when the phone rang one night at ten and the caller ID showed Joe's number, I wasn't surprised.

"Hello, Joe."

"Hey, Chrisy. I hope I didn't wake you up. I had to call. I just watched the movie *Click*, and I think you should watch it," he said, excitement in his voice.

"I'm not much of a Sandler fan," I said.

Joe, a die-hard movie fan, had grown up watching slapstick movies; I'd grown up watching the news and *60 Minutes*, so most often our movie tastes were not in sync.

"But it's really good and has a lot of meaning. Adam Sandler plays a workaholic dad who can fast-forward his life—he sees what mistakes he makes and how he can then go back and fix them."

I readjusted the pillow behind my head and sighed as I lay back again. "Too bad you can't do that too, huh? I wish you could. God, I do. But life is not a movie, Joe."

Mean thoughts and words ricocheted around my brain as I held the receiver to my ear. There were so many things I could say right now to remind him of what he did, how awful he was, the foolish things he'd said when his infidelities were uncovered. But I held my tongue. It wouldn't do any good.

He was extending an olive branch. Again. He'd been doing that a long time now. I had to decide if I wanted to reach for it. He'd been hinting for months that we should not only have peace but give our relationship another try, maybe start dating again. And the crazy thing is, I wanted to. How completely insane was that? It was one thing to be friends again, but it was totally another to be a couple again.

I turned over on my side and faced the side of the bed where he used to sleep. I missed his warm body next to me. I missed snuggling and spooning in the middle of the night. I thought back to when we were first living together—then and for many years afterward, we used to spoon every night, lying with our bodies cupped into each other. We also showered together every single morning for years.

That ended when Dylan came into the world. Life changes in so many ways when you bring another person into the world and into your relationship.

I reached out my hand and rubbed it along the soft, cool sheets where Joe used to sleep. I then ran my hand up toward the pillow where Simba lay. My little Simba, an eight-pound Shih Tzu–Yorkie mix, had been my best little buddy over the past two years, my constant companion. He lifted his head up and leaned in to lick my face, bad breath and all.

I laughed. "Okay, I'll watch the movie, Joe. Now, I have a request for you. Will you go to counseling with me? No matter what happens, I need to talk about us. I need to talk more about what happened and about my frustrations in our marriage. You weren't the only one who was unhappy at times. There were times that I was unhappy and frustrated too, but that goes with the territory. It's not easy being married."

"I know. Marriage is hard. I used to think we were the only ones that had problems, but God, I swear since I started talking to people about what happened to us, everyone I know has marriage problems. And most people's problems are worse than ours were."

"Yeah, too bad you didn't talk to them about it before. We had it pretty good, you know." My wounds were beginning to hurt again and I didn't want to say something I would regret. "I gotta go."

I hung up the phone and turned back over to snuggle with Simba. Was I out of my mind to think about trying this again? How could I ever really trust him? And what would people think?

Scorned women on the *Oprah Winfrey Show* or the news came to my mind. I thought of how I used to despise those women. I thought they were weak, the women who "stood by their men" even after those men had cheated on them. I'd been so disappointed when Hillary Clinton—a strong, intelligent, accomplished woman—took Bill back even when the whole world knew what he'd done. There were countless others. *Come on, get a spine*, I'd think. *Leave that asshole.*

And now I might be one of them. What would people think? I'd told so many people about what had happened to us. Too many. But

I guess I was finally at point in my life where I truly didn't care what people thought of me—one of the nice things about getting older.

I also knew in my heart that I wasn't weak. *I am not weak. I am strong and I am brave.* My friend Lory told me that one time, and it was one of the nicest things anyone had ever said to me. It was a girls' night out and we were talking about what one word we would use to describe each other. Lory said "brave" when describing me.

Katie told me that too in some of her letters. "Thank you for being brave, Mom," she'd said. *But I don't know.* Was considering giving Joe a second chance really brave? Or was it just plain stupid? I didn't know what it was, but I had to give it a try. I didn't want to wake up one day years from now and regret that I never tried to bring us and our family back together.

CHAPTER 59

Michelle, our counselor, said that I didn't need to label this exploration of getting back together as brave or crazy or anything at all. It was healthy and helpful for us to be talking, and Joe, who'd long had an aversion to counselors, actually liked talking with Michelle. She had this incredible gift of listening to us, correctly analyzing and evaluating, and then suggesting.

Joe and I started attending weekly counseling sessions, followed by lunch. They were nice dates, and even though I was still scared at times of what I was doing, I knew that if I did not at least try this that I would someday regret it. I had to at least try.

It's hard to unravel the tangled web of a dozen years of marriage—the love and pain and joy and frustration and ups and downs that come along with it. We'd had a dozen years of fun and excitement—weddings, anniversaries, jobs, travel, friends, parties, promotions, buying a house, getting a dog, and having children. All of this, though, was mixed in with equal or more parts of the mundane and hard work—child-rearing, work stress, laundry, yardwork, housework, paying bills, not getting enough sleep, fights about stupid things, and everything else in between. How do you unravel all of that?

Essentially, Joe said he had wanted more attention in our marriage; essentially, I had wanted more emotional connection and more help around the house and with the kids. He felt I didn't make him a priority. I felt he didn't carry his weight in our marriage, that he only wanted the good and never wanted to talk about the bad or the difficult. He used to tell me, "It should be like a movie," which I could never understand. We both felt that the other person didn't listen to our concerns. Communication had completely broken down over the years.

Two years after we split up, Joe still didn't like talking about the affair. It was in the past and he wanted to keep it there—locked tightly in the chest of times past. I wanted to open it up and dig, but each time it still hurt to look at what was inside. His explanation for keeping the lies going and not admitting guilt and sorrow when I first found out was that he wanted to protect me from further pain. He said that it didn't do any good to tell the truth because it would just hurt me more.

Counseling helped. Eventually our counseling sessions followed by lunch dates turned into evening dates and dinner with friends and bottles of wine. One night following Dylan's baseball game, we invited the family of one of the other players over so that the kids could play and the adults could talk and relax over a few drinks. The kids had a ball playing; we had fun talking, and one drink led to more. By the time our friends left and we cleaned up and put the kids to bed, it was nearly midnight. Joe ended up staying the night.

Two years after we separated, we made love in our bed, in our house, with our boys sleeping just down the hall. It was familiar, comforting, and exciting to reconnect in a physical way and to wake up and have him next to me in the morning.

"I love you so much, 'oney," he said as he kissed me and playfully used the name we'd shared with each other for a dozen years.

"I'm glad you're here, Joe," I said, smiling in return, and quickly entered Mom mode. "Maybe you should leave. Or at least get dressed and go downstairs and act like you just came back over this morning." I started freaking out a little bit. What would the boys do or think? Did this mean I was totally committed again? Were we officially back together?

Before we had time to decide, there was knock on the door. "Mommy, let me in," Jared's little voice said from the other side of the door.

We looked at each other, wide-eyed, and flew out of bed to grab and quickly put on some clothes. Simba's tail started wagging as I walked over and opened the door, wondering how the hell I was going to explain this to Jared.

"Good morning, sweetie," I said to Jared as he burst into the room.

"Hi, Mommy. Hi, Daddy," Jared said without missing a beat as he walked in the room. A huge smile spread across his face. He quickly climbed into bed and said to Joe: "Did you have a sleepover with Mommy?"

"Yes, I did," Joe said, eyes sparkling.

I crawled back into bed—moments later, Dylan walked in the room and also greeted Joe with a "Hi, Daddy," and overall *this is cool* reaction. He climbed into bed as if it were the most natural thing in the world.

So there we lay, all four of us—five, with the dog—snuggling and laughing in our crowded queen-sized bed.

CHAPTER 60

August 2007

I stood in the back of the crowded chapel, looking out at the hundreds of guests who filled the room. The chapel hummed with happy voices, love, energy, and good wishes, and I was so excited—not nervous at all, just excited.

I had to pinch myself at the reality. In just four years since reuniting with Katie, I'd gone from being mother of a daughter to mother of the bride.

"Ready to go, Mom?" asked ten-year-old Dylan as he bent his elbow and turned toward me, looking so handsome and grown up in his dark grey suit and blue tie. His sun-streaked blonde hair accented blue eyes that sparkled with excitement.

"Yes, I'm ready!" I said as I took hold of his arm and admired him, amazed by his maturity and his pride at having a role in his sister's wedding.

I turned then to look at Cindy, dressed in a floor-length dark blue gown that accented her blue eyes. She looked lovely. I was used to seeing her wearing very casual clothes and Birkenstocks on her feet.

"Are you ready too, other mother?" I asked.

"You bet I am," Cindy said with a smile. She took Dylan's other arm, and we began our walk down the chapel aisle.

"Woo-hoo, way to go Cindy!" cheered some friends as we started walking. They were doing some friendly teasing of Cindy, who always dressed casually. It was one of the many things I loved about her—she truly cared what was on the inside, not the outside, and she'd raised our daughter to be the same way.

Beaming with pride, Katie's two mothers and her little brother walked down the aisle of the packed chapel at the church camp where Katie and Paul had met. Sunbeams streamed in through the windows, illuminating the already shining room, and Green Lake in the distance rounded out the picture-perfectness of it all.

As we sauntered past all the smiling faces, I glanced toward Becky, seated to our left, and thanked her in my mind for making all of this possible. For helping me bring Katie into the world, for finding the Schultzes, for being an amazing sister, friend, and aunt. We caught each other's eye and I winked at her. She was sitting next to Joe, who was beaming at the sight of Dylan and me linked arm in arm.

Dylan, with his head tilted high and a smile spread across his face, walked us to the front row, where my mom was already seated next to Katie's other grandma and grandpa.

"Thank you, Dylan," I whispered. "You did a great job."

"No problem, Mom," he said, with all the cool confidence a ten-year-old can muster.

I sat down next to my mother and squeezed her hand, again mentally thanking her for loving me and Katie so much, for always being there, for always supporting me, for being the best mom and grandma.

We turned our heads and looked back down the aisle to watch seven-year-old Jared carry out his duties as ring bearer. He was so excited to have this important job—he took it seriously and held the pillow very steady as he carefully made his way toward the front of the church. He did his best to ignore the flower girl as she cried, wanting nothing to do with her job. She ran as Jared walked smoothly down the aisle, grinning from ear to ear.

"Great job!" I whispered in his ear as he climbed into my lap. "That was perfect, Jared. Just perfect. Now, here comes Katie."

We stood up as the wedding march began to play and looked to our left, where Katie and Dennis stood at the top of the staircase looking down at the congregation.

"She looks so pretty," Jared said as he leaned into me.

Yes, she was pretty—more than that, she was radiant. Katie was absolutely glowing, the picture of elegance and grace with her chic, simple off-the-shoulder dress and swept-up hair. Her dimples accentuated her happiness, like exclamation points written boldly on her face.

"That's our girl," I leaned over and whispered to Cindy, who smiled as the tears spilled down her cheeks. She plucked two Kleenex out of the full-sized box that she held in her hands—that someone had given her as a joke—and handed them to me to wipe my tears.

As Katie and Dennis slowly waltzed down the staircase and the aisle, I recalled the stories Katie had shared with me over the years about the great friendship and bond that she and Dennis had and the things they used to do. When Katie had a bad day when she was little, her Daddy would take her to Walgreens to buy lip gloss and barrettes. When she got older, they'd go to the mall and shop for clothes, go out for lunch, or go for long walks together. In college they'd talk on the phone for hours. I was so happy she had that. It went far beyond the relationship I'd had with my dad. Oh, how I wished my dad could have been here with us today, but I was grateful that they had met and hugged and got to know one another, at least a little bit.

I brought myself back to the ceremony and watched Dennis choke back his tears as he kissed his daughter and hugged his new son-in-law before leaving them at the altar. Katie and Paul took one another's hands and looked deeply into each other's eyes as the ceremony began. Their love was strong and obvious. Despite their young age, they were incredibly mature and deeply spiritual, and it showed.

"Katie has always been special and was always meant to do great things," said Pastor Debbie, who had come from Milwaukee to perform the ceremony. She'd known Katie since she was a baby—baptized her, confirmed her, and allowed her to organize an entire church service when she was in high school. Pastor Debbie knew my girl very well.

"From the time you were in Chrisy's womb, God had great plans for you," she continued, and with that my slow-flowing tears of joy turned into a few sobs—cries from the memory of the pain of letting her go, but mostly cries of immense joy that I brought her into this world, an expression of the pride and honor I felt for the beautiful young woman she had become.

We watched as Katie and Paul gazed into each other's eyes and repeated their vows of love and fidelity to each other. And I thought again and again how lucky I was to be here. I closed my eyes periodically throughout the ceremony and pictured Katie as the little girl I watched grow up in photographs. I'd missed her first words and her first steps. I had missed her birthday parties and school conferences, dance recitals and school plays. I had missed so much.

But I was here today, at the culmination of all those things. All the experiences and people that surrounded her had gotten her to where she was today—this beautiful young woman on the happiest day of her life.

We watched then as they exchanged their rings and the pastor said to Paul, "You may kiss the bride." As their lips touched, Jared exclaimed, "Ooh la la," loudly and clearly. Laughter erupted from the entire congregation. It was a perfect end to the ceremony.

The reception and dance were held in a room adjacent to the chapel, complete with touches of Paul's homeland. Tiny woven baskets from the Maori culture were filled with chocolates and set on the tables. New Zealand and American flag pins were attached to the name cards. New Zealand's signature Sauvignon Blanc was served at every table. Paul and his mates also did the traditional Haka, a dance of the Maori peoples. With their feet spread wide and stomping, their tongues wagging and with loud chanting, Paul, his father, grandfather, brother, and friends performed this Maori warrior dance. We laughed and cheered at the robust performance.

"Another New Zealand tradition," Paul's father explained, "is that people close to the couple give speeches as a way to honor them. So parents, siblings, and friends will be giving speeches up here, and you're more than welcome to do so as well."

Paul's father kicked things off before Dennis and Cindy came up together and read a clever poem they had written about Katie and Paul. Next were more family members and members of the wedding party. Katie and Paul sat at the head table, beaming as they listened to stories about themselves from people who loved them so much. I took in all the wonderful things said about my daughter and her

new husband, picturing them in those first days of meeting here at the camp on the edge of Green Lake, where the buildings are nestled amongst hundred-foot oak trees in the quiet surroundings. Paul told us of the first time he spotted Katie here, and how he was immediately smitten with her.

I was getting to know more about each of them, listening to these stories. And I had a strong urge to say something myself. Yes, I needed to say something. No one had told me about this part of the reception, so I didn't have anything prepared, but I knew I had to do this.

When there was finally a break in the speakers, I took my chance and walked directly to the microphone, my heart beating fast and strong. After scanning the audience and taking a deep, calming breath to slow my rapidly beating heart, I began:

"Hi everyone. I'm Chrisy. I've had the pleasure of meeting many of you, and for those I haven't met yet, I'm Katie's birth mother. Usually if I give a speech, I have practiced it many, many times. Not today. I'm totally winging it here, but I just felt I had to take this opportunity to say how proud I am of Katie and how excited I am to have Paul for a son-in-law. I just feel so very blessed.

"Twenty-two years ago, I took a giant leap of faith when I placed Katie for adoption with Dennis and Cindy. And I must say that out of the six billion people in the world—give or take a few—I couldn't have found better people to be the parents of my child. They are wonderful, special people, and Katie is a wonderful, beautiful person. And I'm just so happy to be part of this, happy to meet all of you who are so important to Katie's life. Here's a toast to Katie and Paul. I love you!"

CHAPTER 61

November 2008
Her ponytail bobbed up and down and waved back and forth to me as I followed behind her, striding along the quiet country road. Her slim, agile figure was framed by lush green pastures that were dotted white with grazing sheep—like a polka-dotted tablecloth draping the landscape. Mesmerized, I watched my daughter run in front of me as we made our morning jog near Arrowtown, New Zealand.

Again, I felt like the luckiest woman in the world. Not only was I in one of the most beautiful places in the world with my daughter and my mom, but back at home, Joe was closing on the sale of his house and moving back in with me and the boys. Yes, I felt incredibly fortunate, if a little bit nervous.

Katie slowed her pace and I caught up with her as we approached the paths next to the river in Arrowtown, an old mining town made somewhat famous by the nearby filming of the *Lord of the Rings* movies. Our jog ebbed to a walk and soon we joined hands, walking slowly along the river basin that was bursting with purple and pink Lupine flowers set against the lush foothills. My seventy-two-year-old mother and I had made the eight-thousand mile journey to New Zealand to visit our girl and her adopted homeland a year after she and Paul had moved back here. They were here so he could complete his college degree.

Side by side and hand in hand, Katie and I ambled along the riverbank discussing our fortune—three generations together in this beautiful country, home to some of the most pristine and beautiful landscapes in the world. With just four million people and forty million sheep, there is a calming, quiet nature about New Zealand. It was the perfect setting for three generations to be together. What struck me most was that the country's beauty was illuminated by a natural light that enhanced the clarity and definition of everything. It was as if I had needed glasses my whole life and was finally seeing with twenty-twenty vision.

"It's good to have you here and to be reminded of how beautiful it is; it's easy to take it for granted after you've been around for a while. You were right in that it is different when you're living and working here," Katie said. "It's been a good year but a hard year; I struggled a lot, but I didn't want to tell you because I didn't want you to think I'd failed."

"Oh, sweetheart. I'd never think that. It's not failure, it's called growing up and becoming an adult. That's hard, especially when you are away from your support system."

I put my arms around her and pulled her toward me. "I'm so proud of you, so incredibly proud. And although living and working here is hard at times, there are millions of people who would die for a chance to do something like this. It's pretty cool."

After months of searching when she first got to the country, Katie had found a job in the accounting department of a plumbing fixtures company. Not a dream job, but work nonetheless in an uncertain economy. It would have to do, and she was working hard and learning about the joys and challenges of being a working adult.

We walked some more and came to the halfway point on the footbridge that spanned the shallow river. We leaned with our elbows on the railing and peered over the side, gazing into the clear, clean water.

Back at our hotel a few hours later, we found Grandma still in her pajamas, practicing yoga on the small patio that overlooked the pristine golf course and the mountains in the distance. "Ah, Grandma, you are so cute and so cool," Katie said, her face beaming.

My mother's arms were raised above her head in sun salutation, and a smile spread across her calm, peaceful face. She had been doing yoga for over twenty years now, since way before it was cool. "I always say yoga saved my life," she said as she moved from sun salutation into downward dog. "And it's what keeps me young."

I smiled at this and was so thankful that Katie was getting to spend this precious time with her grandma. How true it was that yoga had such a profound impact on my mom's life. It helped her become stronger, not only physically but emotionally as well. She was more confident and complete, more independent than when I was growing up. She had a peaceful presence.

After a few days of being spoiled by our stay at the Milbrook Resort, we traveled to Milford Sound via bus and were awed by the magnitude of this incredible natural beauty. Rudyard Kipling once described Milford Sound as "the eighth wonder of the world."

As we neared the sound, we were surrounded by massive, black, jagged rocks tinted green with moss and lined with waterfalls that drizzled down the sides, like white frosting over a dark chocolate cake. Fog hung on the very tops of the mountains, like a veil protecting the full beauty of its bride.

Once in the sound, we boarded the *Milford Wanderer*, a thirty-passenger boat where we would explore the sound and stay overnight. As the *Wanderer* meandered deeper into the sound, the majesty of it all became even more apparent. We were a tiny vessel in a gigantic rock cathedral, where mountains rose nearly five thousand feet on either side of us and waterfalls were everywhere.

Literally dozens and dozens of waterfalls were everywhere we turned. Some were small, elegant trickles of water cascading down the sides of the jagged mountains. Others were big and bold, crashing loudly into the calm waters. A cool mist covered our faces and the air was alive with energy. God, I was so blessed. *Thank you, God. Thank you, universe.*

After a few hours winding through the Sound, our captain anchored the boat where we would stay for the night. Our backdrop was the stunning Mitre Peak, a snowcapped mountain that rose over a mile above the water. It was the most photographed mountain in New Zealand, and there was no question as to why. It was powerful and peaceful at the same time. It was nature in its finest glory, untouched and unspoiled. Katie, my mom, and I stood arm in arm on the deck of our little ship admiring it, appreciating it.

We then had a chance to get up close to the mountainsides that stood all around us. Katie and I joined a group on a small, motorized boat that took us so close we could see the intricate patterns in the rock carved by moving glaciers thousands of years ago. As we made our way back to the Wanderer, a pod of dolphins greeted us, darting in and out of the water in what seemed like a synchronized swimming show.

After Milford Sound, the next and last stop of our journey was Lake Ohau—part of the Teal Lakes area, aptly named for their intense teal blue color and pristine clarity.

As we left the lush, vibrant area of Queenstown, we watched the landscape slowly change into a desolate and barren countryside, beautiful in its own right. When we arrived at Lake Ohau Lodge, it was like stepping back in time. The décor had not been touched or tampered with since at least the 1970s and had the incredible charm and ease of simpler times. There were no TVs and no internet service, just nature and a few people. The restaurant featured a huge, open fireplace, deer heads mounted on the walls, and long wooden tables. There was also a bar and some comfy furniture to curl up on.

After dinner, we took our wine to relax in the living room area where well-worn couches were set against the floor-to-ceiling windows that exposed the lake and the mountains. Magazines, books, and board games—most of them decades old—filled the tables. Good vibes also filled this room. You could feel the spirits of many happy people and the good times that had been enjoyed here.

Katie and Grandma sat on a loveseat with the lake and mountains behind them; I sat quietly across from them, watching and listening as they talked about being together, about how much they loved being granddaughter and grandmother, about how much they and we were alike, how we had the same mannerisms and views, how we loved the same things: the outdoors, the mountains, reading, walking, and what mattered most to us—family, friends, faith.

"We are soul mates," Katie said as she and her grandmother embraced. "You and me and Chrisy, we are all soul mates."

"Oh, yes we are, sweetheart; we are indeed soul mates," Grandma said. "I always knew we'd all be together again someday."

I snapped a picture of them deep in their embrace, Katie's head tucked snuggly against my mother's, their arms locked around each other's backs. Then I joined them, wrapping my arms around both of them. We were intertwined in body, mind, and spirit; mother, daughter, granddaughter.

We had carried each other in our wombs, and we held each other every day in our hearts and in our souls. We shared each other's joy and pain, triumphs and sorrows. We loved each other with every cell and fiber of our being. We three were one. And we kept repeating those three words to each other: "I love you!"

EPILOGUE

I don't know what the odds are—I've never been good at math—but I do know that it is highly unlikely that I would arrive in New Zealand, after twenty-four hours of traveling more than eight thousand miles, to find my daughter, whom I'd placed for adoption nearly three decades ago, in the early stages of labor.

Katie's due date was April 27, 2015. When planning the trip, I didn't want to arrive too early and then use up precious vacation time waiting for the baby's arrival, so I picked a week after her due date to arrive. It was a good guess.

Alex, Katie's friend, picked me up from the airport that morning, and we chatted nonstop on the hour-and-a-half drive from Auckland to Katie and Paul's house in Hamilton. Katie emerged from her front door—before I'd even shut the car door she announced with excitement and trepidation, "I think my water broke!" What are the odds?

After a visit to the midwife and making a few other arrangements, we arrived at Waikato Hospital in Hamilton. It was a public healthcare facility, which meant there were no frills. No artwork on the walls, no comfortable couches or chairs to sit on, no TVs. Only the necessities. It reminded me of what the US hospitals would have looked like in the 1950s—white, stark, utilitarian. But it was free, and it was accessible to everyone in New Zealand.

As Katie's active labor progressed, Paul and I stood on either side of her and held her hands. We offered her encouragement as she pushed and rested and pushed and rested. I watched the miracle unfolding as Katie worked to bring another human being into the world—another human being directly connected to me, to my mother, to my sister.

Watching Katie perform this arduous task of labor carried me back to the delivery room in Ogden, Utah, where I was giving birth to her, with Becky by my side, holding my hand, encouraging me not to give up, to keep pushing. I remembered vividly that final push that separated Katie from my body and the simultaneous feelings of tremendous relief and deep despair. I remembered seeing her perfect face, her perfect arms and legs, her hands, her ten tiny fingers and toes. I remembered wrapping my arms around her and telling her hello and goodbye in the same breath.

It was a miracle that I was here now, watching my daughter give birth to her own. I cheered her on as she gave that final push that brought Remy Mae into the world.

"Here she is!" we said and breathed a sigh of relief. It was instantly replaced with a breath of concern.

Remy had flawlessly formed arms and legs, fingers and toes, and a beautiful little face. Her little body was impeccably designed, but it was covered in a grayish-green slime whose color she matched. She lay on the bed between Katie's legs and was too still. My eyes focused on her chest and strained to see if she was breathing. I could see her chest faintly moving, but something was not right.

The midwife calmly asked me to push the red button above the bed. Within a few seconds, a doctor and two nurses rushed into the room and grabbed the baby. They took her to a table just a few steps away and began sucking at her nose and her mouth and rubbing her body. She was quiet.

We were quiet. We were scared. The medical team talked in hushed voices as Paul and I paced back and forth near them and met each other's eyes with concern. Katie watched from the bed and kept asking, "Is she okay? What's going on? Is she okay?"

"There was a bit of meconium in the amniotic fluid, love," explained the midwife. "That means she took her first poo already. We just want to make sure she didn't ingest any of it."

Mom, please help us here. Please send your healing energy. Silently I began praying to my mom, whose spirit was always nearby.

She had passed away just four months ago. Katie was giving

Remy the middle name of Mae in honor of great-grandma Donna Mae. I prayed to her, to God, to the universe, and to anyone or anything out there who could help us. *Please let her live. This baby cannot die. She cannot die. Let her live. Remy Mae has to live.*

After losing two babies before they were even born, Katie needed and deserved this baby. Her first pregnancy had ended in a miscarriage at ten weeks and was devastating. When the phone rang that morning nearly two years ago and my caller ID said it was from Katie, I knew something was wrong. It was not the right time of day for her to be calling from the other side of the world. She was crushed, and there was nothing I could do to comfort her. I could only assure her that a miscarriage meant something was not right with the baby, and that she would get pregnant again.

She did get pregnant again, and when she made it over the tenuous twelve-week mark everyone breathed a collective sigh of relief. But that didn't last long. A few days later we got the crushing news: an ultrasound revealed the baby had anencephaly—it was missing most of its brain. Katie and Paul were devastated and made the excruciating decision to terminate the pregnancy. How could she possibly carry a child for another six months knowing it would die shortly after birth, if it even made it to that point? Thankfully, she was able to make the choice she made, but it was heartbreaking. This loss was even more harrowing than the first.

She just couldn't take another loss. Nor could I or our family. Not only had Katie lost two babies in the past two years, but we had also lost Becky's son Andrew, just a month shy of his twentieth birthday. After battling mental illness for nearly half his life, Andrew died of an accidental overdose. We were and still are devastated. My heart aches daily for Andrew, for Becky, for her family, for all of us who knew and loved him. He left us far too soon.

We lost my mom just twenty-one months after Andrew died, to congestive heart failure. She died two months before she would have turned eighty and four months before she would have become a great-grandmother. It happened after three days in hospice, surrounded by her children and grandchildren. I was not with her, though, at the moment she took her last breath. She slipped away when I left to go home and shower after spending the night on the floor of her room. The nurse told us it would be a while, many hours or maybe even another day, before she would go, so I left with plans to be back in a little over an hour. As soon as I got home, I got the call from Curt saying, "She's gone." Our beautiful, peaceful, loving mother had taken her last breath.

"We see this a lot," the nurse said, trying to comfort me as soon as I reappeared and verbally flogged myself again and again for having left. "People often let go when someone they are very close to leaves the room. I think that your Mom didn't want to let go when you were here."

I wept as I crawled in bed next to her and caressed the smooth, soft skin of her face and her silky salt-and-pepper hair. I held her petite, buttery-smooth hand and told her over and over again how much I loved her and how much I would miss her.

And oh, how I miss her. She was not only an incredible mother but also an extraordinary human being; she was the most giving, loving person I have ever known. She was my best friend. She was my hero. She loved being a mother and a grandmother, and would have loved being a great-grandmother. Family was everything to her. I remembered the words I wrote for her obituary about her devotion to family and friends and her love of life:

Donna was the consummate homemaker, who created a warm, welcoming, loving home not only for her own family but for anyone who walked through the door—nieces, nephews, neighbors, extended family, and friends. She also created a fun home, allowing her children to experience the joy that all of God's creatures bring. The house was busy not only with friends but a menagerie of pets throughout the years—dogs, litters of puppies, turtles, baby chicks at Easter time, gerbils, tarantulas, and more . . .

Donna also had an amazing sense of adventure throughout her life. She traveled around the world; she slept in a tent next to roaming buffalo;

she rode a mule down the Grand Canyon at age 70 and zip-lined high above the trees in Costa Rica at age 75.

She was also a devoted yoga practitioner and a lifelong learner with an open mind and constant thirst for knowledge and understanding. In addition to Christianity, she was interested in Eastern religions and Native American traditions. Some of the books at her bedside included: The Miracles of Mindfulness, Living Buddha Living Christ, Black Elk Speaks, *and* The Holy Bible. *She was always reading, always learning, always growing.*

Her final words of wisdom for all: "Love, laugh, cry, sing, dance, be kind, be gentle, be compassionate, be good to the Earth, be involved, be (hopefully) registered Democrats. And know that you were not born with a guarantee that life would always be easy . . . sadness stretches the heart so there is more room for joy."

Our hearts had been stretched to their limits and now we were ready for the joy. We needed the bliss, the happiness, and the hope that come when a baby arrives in this world. A baby, fresh, pure, and full of unconditional love and promise.

After a few long and agonizing minutes of diligent work by the medical staff, Remy let out her first cry and her skin began to take on a healthy color. Within a few more minutes, a nurse placed Remy Mae into Katie's arms. I stood at her side, staring at them in reverence. I could have never, ever imagined just how good and amazing and joyful it would all be.

"She is beautiful!"

ACKNOWLEDGEMENTS

This book was nearly thirty years in the making, with more starts and stops than I can count. It's a big slice of my life, so if I know you and you are reading this: Thank you! In some way, big or small, in some shape or form, you touched my life.

People who deserve a special shout-out:

Jane, for your friendships and for always being there, especially when I needed you most.

To Mary Carroll Moore, whose coaching and advice helped me put the real bones and structure to this book nearly a decade ago.

To the fantastic team at Wise Ink Creative Publishing, who helped make this a reality. Thank you for guiding me along on this publishing journey.

To Lory and Koleen, for being such a huge part of the plotline of my life and for thirty years of adventure, fun, and laughter. I have no doubt that fate brought us all to 700 Nicollet Mall so many years ago.

To Jack El-Hai for reading those very first drafts nearly 30 years ago and for the advice, encouragement and friendship along the way.

To Beth and Zoanne, for helping me through the tough "divorce years" when I felt so alone—and mostly for all the adventures and laughs.

To my book club babes, thank you for the highly stimulating literary conversations over the years. Okay, not really. Thanks for the great food, wine, and laughter.

To Steve, my partner in fun and the best "husband" a girl could ever have.

To Nate, for being the best bonus son a mom could ever hope for.

Peace, love, cheers!

BOOK CLUB DISCUSSION QUESTIONS

1. Were you surprised to learn how placing her daughter for adoption impacted so much of Chris's life and who she is?
2. What did you think of Chris's mom's reaction to the news of her pregnancy? What would you say if it were your daughter, or what would your mom say if it were you?
3. Was Chris's decision not to have an abortion driven by her not wanting to disappoint her mom? By her faith? By her nineteenth birthday?
4. When do you think was the toughest time for Chris, from the time she got pregnant to the birth/afterward? Do you think she knew how much she'd grieve for her child?
5. What would be the most important qualities you'd look for in an adopting family?
6. Chris described her sister Becky as her "person." Who is your person?
7. Did this book change your perspective on adoption, parenthood, or the right to choose?
8. What did you learn from this book that you didn't know before?
9. What is the significance of the title? Where else did you see a reference(s) to the title, *Those Three Words*? What other meanings are there besides, "You are pregnant"?
10. There are so many details in the book about Chris's life growing up and going to college. Do you suppose she journaled? Remembered? Did research?

11. Chris realized her dream of writing. What has been one of your dreams? Are you doing it? Did your dreams change?
12. Have you sacrificed a career or dream of doing something because of family/kids/other reasons?

ABOUT THE AUTHOR

Chris Bauer is first and foremost a proud mother and grandmother—of both humans and canines. (Truth be told, there were moments along her motherhood journey when she preferred the canines.)

She is also a writer and marketing professional living in Minneapolis. She has loved words, books, reading, and writing for as long as she can remember. *Those Three Words* is her first book. Visit www.authorcbauer.com for more information.

www.ingramcontent.com/pod-product-compliance
Lightning Source LLC
Chambersburg PA
CBHW060518080526
44586CB00012B/532